THE
MOURNER'S
COMFORTER

CHARLES HADDON SPURGEON

REVIVAL LITERATURE
P.O. BOX 6068
ASHEVILLE, NC 28816
800-252-8896
www.revivallit.org

Scriptures are from the Authorized King James Version of the Bible.

Opine Publishing
Columbia, Maryland 21044 USA
http://www.opinebooks.com
Books for the Thinking Christian – for Life, Family, and Faith
Opinari (L.) – to think, to reason, ...to believe

Publisher's Cataloging-in-Publication

Spurgeon, C. H. (Charles Haddon), 1834-1892.
  The mourner's comforter / Charles Haddon Spurgeon.
  p. cm.
  Includes bibliographical references.
  New ed. of the work previously published: Haywards
Heath, Sussex : Carey Publications, 1975, which is a
reprint of the original: 1st ed. London, 1878.
  ISBN 0-9708451-8-9

  1. Bible. O.T. Isaiah LXI, 1-3--Criticism,
interpretation, etc.   I. Title.

BS1520.5.S68 2007   224'.106
                          QBI07-600064

Gateway Publications, Greensboro, NC, USA , made this edition possible.

Cover design is by Cristina Mershon.

THE
MOURNER'S
COMFORTER

Charles Haddon Spurgeon

June 19,1834 — January 31, 1892

"...what God has done with one life *totally committed* to Him whose power is *unlimited*!"—G.C. Primm [Romans 8:28]

Charles Haddon Spurgeon, born in Kelvedon, Essex, England, was the most well-known and popular preacher of his time. He began preaching at age 19.

At age 20, Mr. Spurgeon was called to the renowned New Park Street Chapel in London. On March 18, 1861, he became the pastor of the Metropolitan Tabernacle, built to accommodate the large crowds seeking to hear him. Audiences numbering up to 6,000 heard him preach on any given Sunday. He relied on prayer—his own and those of the people of his church—and referred to prayer as the church's powerhouse.

Many have called C. H. Spurgeon the greatest modern preacher. He sought to make his messages clear to even the least-educated, yet many prominent figures of England's political and social life of his day went to hear him preach and sought to know him personally.

Devotion to Jesus Christ marked Charles Haddon Spurgeon's life, character, and preaching. His astounding memory, oratorical gifts, and prolific writing continue to be well known around the world. Mr. Spurgeon established a school for preachers, founded an orphanage, and led or supported many philanthropic works.

He and his wife, Susannah Thompson, had twin sons. Although chronic illness kept her much confined at home, she diligently worked to further various helping ministries for the poor of London. She also encouraged the development of a process for the distribution of her husband's writing—a work that grew beyond the couple's expectations.

The Book's Place among Mr. Spurgeon's Works

The Mourner's Comforter, seven discourses on Isaiah 61:1-3, was the fourth of seven books in Spurgeon's Shilling Series. The series was released in 1875. Each book was intended to sell for a shilling, about twelve pennies.

Charles Haddon Spurgeon was a prolific writer of sermons, proverbs, and devotionals. In addition to sixty-three volumes of his *Sermons,* there are three volumes of *The Pulpit Library.* From 1865 until his death in 1892 (27 years), he published *The Sword and the Trowel,* a monthly magazine that dealt with issues of the day affecting the church. A few titles, from among his many works, are listed below:

> *Sermons* – over 60 volumes
> *The Pulpit Library* – three volumes
> *The Shilling Series*
> *The Interpreter*
> *The Clue of the Maze*
> *The Treasury of David*
> *Morning by Morning*
> *Evening by Evening*
> *The Chequebook of the Bank of Faith* (reprinted as
>   *Faith's Checkbook*)
> *The Golden Alphabet of the Praises of Holy Scripture*
> *John Ploughman's Talk*

For many years, Mr. Spurgeon went to Menton, France, for rest and recuperation from recurring health problems, and there he died in his 58th year. Soon after, William Jewell College, Liberty, Missouri, USA, acquired most of Mr. Spurgeon's personal library. The Jewell College Spurgeon Collection is in the Curry Library. The archive includes *The Mourner's Comforter,* as does at least one private collection.

Editorial Remarks about this Edition

This long-awaited new edition of the rare Charles Haddon Spurgeon book, *The Mourner's Comforter*, has seven discourses on Isaiah 61:1-3. Its source is a 1975 reprint of a rare edition of the original. (See Acknowledgements.) The rare source edition remains in a private Spurgeon library. We wish to thank the book's owner and Gateway Publications for allowing this new edition.

Editorial changes stayed close to original expression, modified only to help avoid confusion or distraction for today's readers, due to English language usage changes since the 19th century. Countless hours over a two-year investigation of every word, line, paragraph, and theme of Mr. Spurgeon's text led to the present form. The editors strove to stay true to Mr. Spurgeon's style and meaning. The publisher believes that Mr. Spurgeon's tone, style, and meaning have been preserved.

When approaching language, formatting, and content decisions, the editors' primary and over-riding goal was to keep to the original, word for word, as much as possible. Because of this, some readers may think that certain parts should have been left out or amended. However, we believe that *The Mourner's Comforter* readers should be able to read what Mr. Spurgeon said, rather than what some may think he should or should not have said.

This language-updated edition is not a paraphrase. The authorized King James Version of the Bible, from which Mr. Spurgeon preached, is this edition's Scripture text.

The Contents section of this new edition expanded to include sub-headings that occurred originally only within the text. The editors felt this would help the readers more easily find desired themes. The small caps and italics in this edition appear as they were in the source edition.

The editors replaced archaic words with current words in use, and updated syntax and formatting wherever doing so would greatly enhance reading flow for today's reader.

Examples of word and language substitutions in the author's text are: "you" and "your" replace *thee* and *thy*; "has" replaces *hath*. "Wood" replaces *rood*, an archaic word meaning either cross or crucifix or a unit of measurement equal to a quarter of an acre or a rod (furlong); the author's context suggested the substitution choice. American English spelling replaces British English spelling for words such as *favour*, *Saviour*, and *honour*, to render them, respectively—"favor," "Savior," and "honor."

To avoid interrupting the text with explanations, definitions, and attributions, the editors inserted superscript numbers to refer readers to corresponding notes in the appropriate chapter's list in Reference Notes.

Punctuation frequently follows the original.

Syntax alterations served goals of clarity and necessary conformity with recent English usage. For example, in the original edition, the sentence: "*You find sometimes that the will to do well is present with you, but how to perform that which you would you find not,*" now reads: "You find sometimes that the will to do well is present with you, but you do not find how to perform it."

Pronouns that refer to God have been capitalized, according to U.S. usage. For example, "he" referring to God is presented as "He" in the text. This change also, in some instances, helped avoid uncertainty about pronoun references. The King James Version (KJV) British English style, which does not capitalize pronouns referring to God, has been maintained wherever the KJV is quoted.

The publishing practices of Mr. Spurgeon's day did not require citing sources of prose, poetry, or lyrics. Where Mr. Spurgeon referred to a person or provides a quote, where the source was identifiable, it is now indicated to the extent possible.

Note: Luke 4:18-21 relates and corresponds to Isaiah 61:1-2*a*. Mr. Spurgeon often compared the two texts and commented on their significance.

The Author's Preface

Heavy heart, this book is meant for you. He who sends forth this volume knows the heart of a mourner by a kindred experience, and is most anxious to be a "son of consolation" to the sorrowing. This little volume is meant to scare the night-raven, of which Milton tells us that it sits "where brooding darkness spreads his jealous wings." Most men know it as Religious Melancholy, but we call it by the older and more scriptural name of Mourning in Zion. By whatever name it is called it is none the more pleasant, for truly—

> Its gloomy presence saddens all the scene,
> Shades every flower and darkens every green;
> Deepens the murmur of the falling floods,
> And breathes a browner horror on the woods.

To meet the sadness of the heart we have taken a prescription, not from Galen or Hippocrates, but from the great gospel prophet, Isaiah; and its one and only ingredient is Christ Jesus Himself, who is anointed to comfort the distressed in heart, and fulfils His office by giving Himself to them to meet all their needs. The sermons that make up this book are full of Christ Jesus, the consolation of Israel; and if, in any degree, they cheer the desponding, it will be entirely due to Him, their object and their theme. He is to mourning hearts—

> Sweet as refreshing dews or summer showers
> To the long parching thirst of drooping flowers.

No heart, however broken, needs any balm but Jesus to work its perfect cure. Sorrows, which like Noah's flood drown all, are soon assuaged by a word from His lips. Get Him and keep Him, O bruised and bleeding heart, and you are healed. For broken hearts the broken-hearted Savior died, and for them He lives and pleads. Look to Him, mourner, and the black horror of despair shall end.

Yours heartily,
C. H. Spurgeon

Acknowledgements

Errol Hulse, editor of *Reformation Today* magazine in Liverpool, England, spotted this rare Spurgeon book in my library and was the first to encourage me to republish this work. When I republished it in 1975, he bought hundreds of copies of the first reprint for distribution through his Carey Publications. It again fell out of print. Now, I have allowed Opine Publishing to undertake this new edition.

One can never adequately express appreciation to those who have helped them produce a work of literature. Many who have looked through my extensive library of books and articles by and about Charles H. Spurgeon have been surprised to find some very rare copies of his works and those written about him. For example, in almost any listing of Spurgeon's books you are not likely to find *The Mourner's Comforter*. Why, I do not know. The copy I have was one of thousands that were published in Spurgeon's lifetime. I am truly grateful for the book finder in England, whose name I do not recollect at this time, for finding for me the edition I have had for so many years.

In addition, I must give a very special word of thanks to Sharon Youngmark for retyping this entire manuscript for republication in a more modern type. Without her help it may not have been possible for me to offer this book for republication in its present form.

Carri Hesson, who offered her services in ministry through word processing and publication design for Opine Publishing, has re-formatted the text and assisted with the language updates. I thank her here for her work, done in love for the Lord.

What more can I say? Many who bought the first reprint and profited from it should certainly be mentioned in my acknowledgement of appreciation to those who have helped to resurrect this book for modern readers.

Just the other day I was told by the president of one of the largest seminaries in the world that in his research on Spurgeon he found that Spurgeon is the number one writer in volume of books published in the English language. This, in itself, seems to me encouragement enough to republish this book in a way that will allow it to never go out of print again.

Gerald C. Primm
Editor, *Paradoxes, Mysteries, Riddles, Enigmas, and Comfort for Christians: A Compilation of Selected Charles H. Spurgeon*

Foreword

A reprint of *The Mourner's Comforter* was given to me many years ago. I had no idea then what a profound and blessed gift it was. In those years, problems and unfulfilled desires filled my concentration; I had come to a point of assuming that God did not care about me or was a distant dream of a religious idea. Being done with religion after many failed attempts, I put the little book on one of my crowded bookshelves and forgot about it.

Years later, in depths of sadness and desperation, I was ill and alone at home for many weeks. One day I searched among books in an effort to drive away distressing thoughts. The long-neglected copy of *The Mourner's Comforter* caught my eye. I took the book in hand, turned randomly to one of its pages, and began to read. Themes embraced and comforted me.

Over the many days of tumultuous recuperation, I continued to read and re-read favorite lines, paragraphs, and pages. God faithfully answered my chief distress, as I meditated on Mr. Spurgeon's expositions of the prophetic Scriptures. They helped draw me into the palpable reach of God's divine and life-changing love.

My copy is marked and worn from years of use. Isaiah declared and Jesus fulfilled the powerful message therein presented and explained by a man of remarkable Christian faith, character, preaching, and teaching.

I hope that many readers will accept the balm and strength contained in the messages of this book. Regardless of how often the words of Isaiah 61:1-3 have been heard or studied, here their meanings emerge in a deeper light. Their truth can comfort and restore the willing heart. May God refresh every reader. To Him be the glory, forever.

Jane Bullard [pen name]
Author, *Not All Roads Lead Home—a Story of Renewed Love*

Contents

Isaiah 61:1-3

The Spirit of the Lord GOD is upon me; because the LORD hath anointed me to preach good tidings unto the meek; he hath sent me to bind up the broken-hearted, to proclaim liberty to the captives, and the opening of the prison to *them that are* bound;

To proclaim the acceptable year of the LORD, and the day of vengeance of our God; to comfort all that mourn;

To appoint unto them that mourn in Zion, to give unto them beauty for ashes, the oil of joy for mourning, the garment of praise for the spirit of heaviness; that they might be called trees of righteousness, the planting of the LORD, that he might be glorified.

CHAPTER 1

The Anointed Messenger and His Work

> The Spirit of the Lord GOD is upon me; because the LORD hath anointed me to preach good tidings unto the meek; he hath sent me to bind up the broken-hearted, to proclaim liberty to the captives, and the opening of the prison to them that are bound... —*Isaiah 61:1*

May a dew from the Lord rest upon us while we consider line by line this wonderful passage from what has been well called "the Gospel according to Isaiah." May many who mourn derive consolation from our meditations.

This Scripture is true if applied to everyone whom God has ordained to declare the glad tidings. It was true of Isaiah when he spoke as the great evangelical prophet. It has been true of the apostles and of all who have been enabled in the divine strength to proclaim the testimony of mercy.

The text shows us that the great business of every true minister is to preach the gospel: there are other duties to be fulfilled, but this is the head and front of a minister's calling. Every minister should say, "This one thing I do: the Lord has appointed me to preach good tidings to the meek." The preaching can, however, only be done in the power of a divine anointing. The one who speaks for God should speak in God's strength because the Spirit of God has come upon him, is moving him to speak, is helping him while speaking, and will make the word which he proclaims to be quick and powerful.

To attempt to preach in any power but that of the Holy Spirit is to ensure failure. There can be no broken hearts mended or captives set free where the Spirit of God is not honored. The preacher giving himself up wholly to his preaching, and discharging his work in the power of the Spirit, should aim at the results that are mentioned in the text. He must pity broken hearts and endeavor to bind them up. He must remember the Lord's prisoners and seek their release.

If he does not aim at those outcomes, he forgets the design of true preaching, which is not for preaching's sake, much less for the preacher's sake. Rather, it is all for the sake of the people of God, many of whom Satan holds in bondage under sin. The preacher must never consider that his preaching has succeeded unless he continually hears the joyful cries of liberated captives and the songs of comforted mourners.

While it is true that the text has a meaning towards all God's servants, our Lord has told us that this passage is to be interpreted concerning Himself. When He stood up in the synagogue of Nazareth and read from the scroll these gracious words, He closed the book, gave it to the minister, and added, "This day is this scripture fulfilled in your ears."[1]

That day when He was present, preaching and teaching, was the time in which the text was fulfilled. The fullness of its meaning was turned into matter of fact, for there had come One who above all others was anointed of the Spirit of God that He might proclaim glad tidings to the meek.

We shall, therefore, only consider the text as referring to our blessed Redeemer. We will allow all other teachers to vanish into Him, as the stars merge their light in the rising sun: Christ Jesus is He who comes to bind the broken hearts and to break the iron chains.

Following our text closely, we shall first consider *our Lord's anointing*. He says, "The Spirit of the Lord *is* upon me, because he hath anointed me...." Second, we shall dwell upon *our Lord's preaching*—"The Lord hath anointed me to preach good tidings unto the meek"; and then thirdly, we shall carefully consider *our Lord's design and objective*—"He hath sent me to bind up the broken-hearted, to proclaim liberty to the captives, and the opening of the prison to them that are bound."

I. First, let us contemplate OUR LORD'S ANOINTING.

The first remark under this heading shall be this—*it was very special*. He was anointed of the Spirit first in order, for He is first and chief. He is the head, and on Him the sacred unction first descends, and then to us. Even as the priestly oil was poured upon the head of Aaron, and then flowed down to the skirts of his garments, so is the Spirit first, and originally, given to the Christ of God, and then through Him it falls upon us. Our anointing is a secondary one: because He is Christ we are Christians—the Anointed is surrounded by anointed ones.

Our Lord was specially endowed with the Spirit at the first, for He was born supernaturally, according to the word of the angel to the highly favored virgin: And the angel answered and said to her, "The Holy Ghost shall come upon thee, and the power of the Highest shall overshadow thee: therefore also that holy thing which shall be born of thee shall be called the Son of God."[2]

Mysteriously begotten, our Lord came into the world, and from His childhood He manifested the special possession of the Spirit: for He was filled with wisdom, and the grace of God was upon Him. His actual anointing took place at the time of His baptism. When He came up out of the water, John bore witness that he saw the Spirit descending like a dove and resting upon Him. The Spirit has not in any visible form descended upon us. We, I trust, have received Him, but not in that way. The manifestation belongs exclusively to Him who came to baptize us with the Holy Spirit and with fire.

The special aspect of His anointing lies also in the fact that "God giveth not the Spirit by measure *unto him.*"[3] To us the Spirit is given by measure according to our need. For quickening, for illumination, for sanctification, for the gift of utterance, and various necessary uses, according to our capacity, we receive of the Holy Spirit; but our Lord, having an infinite capacity, received an infinity of the Spirit of God.

Again, there was a special aspect in this—that the Spirit, when He descended upon the Lord Jesus, "abode upon him."[4] The Spirit does not continue at all seasons with every child of God, for sometimes we grieve Him, and He departs from us. We have not always, at any rate, the conscious presence of the Holy Spirit, but John tells us, "He that sent me to baptize with water the same said unto me, Upon whom thou shalt see the Spirit descending, and remaining on him, the same is he which baptizeth with the Holy Ghost."[5]

So you see, dear friends, the anointing of our Lord has the special character of being without equal, without measure, and without withdrawal. Jesus is at no time more anointed than at another, but always full of the Holy Spirit. You and I sometimes have the fullness of the Spirit; at other times we are crying that His Spirit may return to us: but Jesus never grieved the Spirit, nor could He do so, for in Him is no sin.

Next, with regard to the possession of the Spirit by our Lord, it is special, because *He has ordained Him to special offices*, upon which none of us can enter. There are three offices to which men of old were appointed by being anointed— prophet, priest, and king.

First, the prophetical office was received in this way. We read of Elisha, that God said to Elijah, "Go and anoint Elisha, the son of Shaphat, that he may be prophet in thy stead."[6]

Priests, too, were anointed: you have a long series of rules given in the book of Leviticus for the anointing of Aaron and of his sons with an oil that was made according to the art of the apothecary, with choice spices mingled in an unusual manner to make an oil that should never touch the flesh of any man but the high priest. For him and for him alone was the oil of his anointing before God; and so the Lord Jesus is anointed as a priest with the oil of gladness above His fellowmen.

Kings, too, were anointed. Saul was only anointed with a vial of oil, whereas David was anointed with a horn of oil, as if to mark the abundance of his kingdom and the favor in which he stood in the sight of God.

As for our most blessed Lord, He is called the Messiah, or the sent One, and that office includes priesthood, prophecy, and kingship, all in one, and in each of these offices He is plentifully anointed of God.

Would you know the truth? Jesus can teach it to you, for God has given Him the Spirit to be a prophet among us. Would you be cleansed from sin? Christ can remove all impurity by means of His priestly office, for He has presented a complete sacrifice, and He can apply its cleansing power to your soul and make you know that as a priest the fullness of the Spirit dwells with Him. Do you long to have sin conquered? Do you need the aid of supreme power to subdue your corruptions? Christ can exercise it, for He is anointed by the Holy Spirit to be King in the hearts of men.

I delight to think of our blessed Lord in those three offices, each one of which we so much need. I delight to perceive the heavenly perfume that flows from His person and work, because of the holy oil of the Spirit that rests upon Him.

Now, *this anointing produced in our Lord remarkable results*, worthy of being mentioned under this heading. We noticed that the Spirit of God was upon Christ, that He might preach. We must look to His preaching for its effects, and we notice that His utterance as the result of the indwelling of the Spirit was surpassingly powerful. "Never man spake like this man,"[7] said those who went to take Him.

Those who listened to Him were charmed with His accents, and even the ministers of justice who were sent to seize Him, and who are usually the last persons ever to be affected by oratory, nevertheless came under the spell of His words. I should suppose that a sheriff's officer who came to arrest a preacher would be the last person to be impressed by his sermon; yet these men went back to those who sent them and reported that they could not take Him, for no man ever spoke as He did. He was a mighty preacher; He spoke as one having authority.

All other speakers will do well to sit at His feet and learn their art from the great Master of it. No man ever spoke like this man, because the Spirit of God rested upon Him as it has never rested upon another.

The result was seen in His own spirit, for what a spirit dwelled in Jesus Christ. So gentle, He was tender as a nurse with her child. So brave, He never feared the face of man. What strong words are His. How forcible! How courageous! He is a man to the very fullness of manhood, and yet He is always the holy child Jesus. His spirit was unselfish, for the Spirit of God consecrated Him entirely to His work; He lived and died for it. He never thought of self at all, but the zeal of God's house did eat Him up, and He was clothed with zeal as with a cloak.[8]

You never detect in His spirit the imperfections that are so palpable in us. He is never cold or indifferent; His words never freeze on His lips. He is never proud and lofty; you never find Him using language that the poor could not understand, yet, you find Him condescending to people of low estate as if it were no condescension at all.

Above all, His spirit was saturated with love. He looked with love upon those who hated Him, and even when at last He had to give them up to perish, His proclamation of the destruction of Jerusalem was made wet by His tears. He loved our guilty race as men never loved each other. He, the greatest of men, loved His ungrateful people with all His heart, and hence His preaching was so full of power.

And then, as His utterance and spirit were thus full of the Holy Spirit, His whole career became marvelous because of it: Jesus of Nazareth went about doing good, because He was a man filled with the Spirit of God. It was not only what He did and spoke in public. The Spirit of God was as conspicuous in His private prayers. The Spirit inspired not only His proclamations among the crowd, but also His quiet and gentle teaching of the twelve in the lone places, where He told them the secrets of His heart.

The Man Himself was power because of the Spirit. His thoughts, His words, His glances, His sufferings, everything about Him through the power of this anointing became subservient to His great life work. Hence it is that now, though Jesus has gone from us, there remains about His name a wondrous power; and about the truths that He reveals to us there is a sacred might. Since the Spirit of God still rests upon Him, and upon His word, when He is preached His saving work is accomplished in those that believe.

This is the very joy and strength and hope of the church—that the Lord anointed Jesus to preach the gospel, and that His Spirit still goes forth with those who are sent in His name. The Spirit still rests upon the pages of the Bible, in each promise and precept and exhortation, making all to be instinct with life. He still comes upon the members of Christ's mystical body, and in His power that body remains unconquerable.

All the multitudinous iniquities and grievous errors of this world shall yet yield before Christ, because the Spirit of God is almighty and He glorifies Christ. He that brooded over chaos broods over this disordered universe, and He will bring order out of confusion; therefore, we look for a millennium from Him. He that said, "Let there be light," and caused light to spring forth, still lives, and He will still give light to the dark places of the earth, till over the new creation this glorious anointed Christ shall shine forth in His strength like the sun. He shall reign among His ancients gloriously, because the power of the Spirit is upon Him.

II. Second, let us contemplate OUR LORD'S PREACHING. He says, "The Lord hath anointed me to preach good tidings to the meek."

To begin, the anointing was *with a view to preaching.* The Lord puts such honor upon the ministry of the Word that, as one of the old Puritans said, "God had only one Son, and He made a preacher of Him." It should greatly encourage the weakest amongst us, who are preachers of righteousness, to think that the Son of God, the blessed and eternal Word, came into this world that He might preach the same good tidings that we are called to proclaim.

We may profitably note how earnestly our Lord kept to His work. It was His business to preach, He did preach, and He was always preaching. "What," you say, "did He not work miracles?" Yes, but the miracles were sermons; they were acted discourses, full of instruction.

He preached when He was on the mountains; He equally preached when He sat at the table in the Pharisee's house. All His actions were significant; He preached by every movement. He preached when He did not speak; His silence was as eloquent as His words. He preached when He gave, and He preached when He received; for He was preaching a sermon when He lent His feet to the woman, that she might wash them with her tears and wipe them with the hairs of her head, quite as much as when He was dividing the loaves and the fishes and feeding the multitude.

He preached by His patience before Pilate, for there He witnessed a good confession. He preached from the bloody tree: with hands and feet fastened there, He delivered the most wonderful discourse of justice and of love, of vengeance and of grace, of death and of life, that was ever preached in this poor world.

O, yes, He preached. He was always preaching; with all His heart and soul He preached. He prayed that He might obtain strength to preach. He wept in secret that He might the more compassionately preach the word that wipes men's tears away. Always a preacher, He was always ready in season and out of season with a good word. As He walked the streets He preached as He went along; and if He sought seclusion, and the people thronged Him, He did not send them away without a gracious word.

This was His one calling, and this one calling He pursued in the power of the eternal Spirit. He liked it so well, and thought so much of it, that He trained His eleven friends and sent them out to preach too. Then He chose seventy more for the same errand, saying, "As you go, preach the gospel."[9]

Did He shave the head of one of them to make him a priest? Did He decorate one of them with a gown, a chasuble, or a biretta? Did He teach one of them to say mass—to swing a censer or to elevate the host? Did He instruct one of them to regenerate children by baptism? Did He bring them up to chant in surplices and march in procession?

No, those things He never thought of, and neither will we. If He had thought of them it would only have been with utter contempt, for what is there in such childish things?

The preaching of the cross is foolishness to those that perish, but unto us who are saved, it is the wisdom of God and the power of God; for it pleases God by the foolishness of preaching to save them that believe.[10]

As our Lord ascended He said, "Go ye into all the world, and preach the gospel to every creature."[11] His charge in brief was: "Preach, preach, even as I have done before you."

Now, as you have seen that our Savior came to preach, notice *His subject.* "The Lord...hath anointed me to preach *good tidings* to the meek." And what good tidings did He preach? Pardon, pardon given to the chief of sinners, pardon for prodigal sons pressed to their father's bosom. Restoration from their lost estate, as the piece of money was restored again into the treasury, and the lost sheep back to the fold.

How encouragingly He preached of a life given to men dead in sin, life through the living water, which becomes a fountain within the soul. You know how sweetly He would say, "He that believeth in me, though he were dead, yet shall he live."[12] "And as Moses lifted up the serpent in the wilderness, even so must the Son of Man be lifted up; that whosoever believeth in Him should not perish, but have everlasting life."[13]

He preached a change of heart and the need of a new creation. He said, "Ye must be born again,"[14] and He taught those truths by which the Holy Spirit works in us and makes all things new. He preached glad tidings concerning resurrection, and bade men to look for endless bliss by faith in Him. He cried, "I am the resurrection and the life. He that liveth and believeth in me shall never die."[15]

He gave forth precepts, too, and warnings in their place. Some of them were very searching and severe, but they were only used as accessories to the good news. He made men feel that they were poor, so that they might be ready to be rich. He made them feel weary and burdened, so that they might come to Him for rest; but the sum and substance of what He preached was the gospel—the good spell—the glad news.

Brothers, our divine Lord always preached upon that subject, and did not stoop to secular themes. If you notice, although He would sometimes debate with Pharisees, Herodians, and others, as needs required, yet He was soon away from them and back to His one theme. He baffled them with His wisdom, and then returned to the work He loved, namely, preaching where the publicans and sinners drew near to hear Him.

Our business, since the Spirit of God is upon us, is not to teach politics, except as these immediately touch the kingdom of Christ, and there the gospel is the best weapon. Nor is it our business to be preaching mere morals, and rules of duty; our ethics must be drawn from the cross, and begin and end there. We are to declare not so much what men ought to do, as to preach the good news of what God has done for them.

Nor must we always be preaching certain doctrines as doctrines, apart from Christ. We are only theologians so far as theology enshrines the gospel. We have one thing to do, and to that one thing we must keep. The old proverb says, "Shoemaker, stick to your pattern";[16] depend upon it, that is good advice to the Christian minister—to stick to the gospel and make no move away from it.

I hope I have always kept to my theme, but I take no credit for it, for I know nothing else. I have "determined to know nothing among men, save Jesus Christ and Him crucified."[17] Indeed, necessity is laid upon me; indeed, woe be unto me if I preach not the gospel. I would gladly have but one eye, and that eye capable of seeing nothing from the pulpit but lost men and the gospel of their salvation: to all else one may well be blind, so that the entire force of the mind may center on the great essential subject.

There is, certainly, enough in the gospel for any one man, enough to fill any one life, to absorb all our thought, emotion, desire, and energy; yes, there is infinitely more than the most experienced Christian and the most intelligent teacher will ever be able to bring forth. If our Master kept to His one topic, we may wisely do the same, and if any say that we are narrow, let us delight in that blessed narrowness which brings men into the narrow way. If any denounce us as cramped in our ideas and confined to one set of truths, let us rejoice to be confined with Christ, and count it the truest enlargement of the mind.

It would be good to be bound with cords to His altar, to lose all hearing but for His voice, all seeing but for His light, all life but in His life, all glorying save in His cross. If He who knew all things taught only the one necessary thing, His servants may rightly enough do the same. "The Lord hath anointed me," He said, "to preach good tidings," and in this anointing let us abide.

Now notice *the persons* to whom He especially addressed the good tidings. They were the meek. Just look at the fourth chapter of Luke, and you will read there, "The Lord hath anointed me to preach the gospel to the poor"! The poor, then, are among the persons intended by "the meek." I noticed when I was looking through this passage that the Syriac[18] renders it "the humble," and I think the Vulgate[19] translates it "the gentle." Calvin translates it "the afflicted."

It all comes to one thing—the meek, a people who are not lofty in their thoughts, for they have been broken down; a people who are not proud and lifted up, but low in their own esteem; a people who are often much troubled and tossed about in their thoughts; a people who have lost proud hopes and self-conceited joys; a people who seek no high things, crave no honors, desire no praises, but bow before the Lord in humility.

They are willing to creep into any hole to hide, because they have such a sense of insignificance and worthlessness and sin. They are a people who are often desponding, and are apt to be driven to despair. The meek, the poor—meek because they are poor: they would be as bold as others if they had as much as others, or as much as others think they have; but God has emptied them, and so they have nothing of which to boast.

They feel the iniquity of their nature, the plague of their hearts; they mourn that in them there dwells no good thing, and often they think themselves to be rubbish. They imagine themselves to be more brutish than anyone, and quite beneath the Lord's regard; sin weighs them down, and yet they accuse themselves of insensibility and impenitence. To such as these, the Lord has anointed the Lord Jesus on purpose to preach the gospel.

If any of you are good and deserving, if any of you are keeping God's law perfectly and hope to be saved by your works, then the gospel is not for you. The healthy have no need of a physician. The Lord Jesus did not come upon so needless an errand as that of healing those who have no wounds or diseases.

However, the sick need a doctor, and Jesus has come in great compassion to remove their sicknesses. The more diseased you are, the more sure you may be that the Savior came to heal such as you are. The more poor you are, the more certain you may be that Christ came to enrich you; the more sad and sorrowful you are, the more sure you may be that Christ came to comfort you.

You nobodies, you who have been turned upside down and emptied right out, you who are bankrupt and begging, who feel yourselves to be clothed with rags and covered with wounds, bruises, and putrefying sores, who are utterly bad through and through, and know it, and mourn it, and are humbled about it—you may rightly feel that God has poured the holy oil without measure upon Christ on purpose that He might deal out mercy to such poor creatures as you are.

What a blessing this is! How we ought to rejoice in the Lord's anointing, since it benefits such despicable objects. We who feel that we are such objects ought to cry, "Hosanna, blessed is he that cometh in the name of the Lord."[20]

III. Our third and last major theme upon this text is—OUR LORD'S DESIGN AND OBJECTIVE in thus preaching the gospel to the poor and the meek. Observe that it was, first, so that He might *bind up the broken-hearted.* "He hath sent me to bind up the broken-hearted." Carefully heed this purpose, so that you may see whether it belongs to you.

Are you broken-hearted because of sin, because you have sinned often, foully, and grievously? Are you broken-hearted because your heart will not break, as you would desire it would break; broken-hearted because you repent that you cannot repent as you would, and grieved because you cannot grieve enough? Are you broken-hearted because you have not such a sense of sin, as you ought to have, and such a deep loathing of it, as you perceive that others have?

Are you broken-hearted with despair as to self-salvation; broken-hearted because you cannot keep the law; broken-hearted because you cannot find comfort in ceremonies; broken-hearted because the things which looked best have turned out to be deceptions; broken-hearted because all the world over you have found nothing but broken cisterns which hold no water, which have mocked your thirst when you have gone to them; broken-hearted with longing after peace with God?

Are you broken-hearted because prayer does not seem to be answered; broken-hearted because when you come to hear the gospel you fear that it is not applied to you with power; broken-hearted because you had a little light and yet slipped back into the darkness?

Are you broken-hearted because you are afraid you have committed the unpardonable sin; broken-hearted because of blasphemous thoughts which horrify your mind and yet will not leave it?

I care not why or wherefore you are broken-hearted, for Jesus Christ came into the world, sent of God with this objective—to bind up the broken-hearted. It is a beautiful figure, this binding up—as though the crucified One took the healing ointment with the bandages and put it around the broken heart—and with His own dear gentle hand proceeded to close up the wound and make it cease to bleed.

Luke does not tell us that the Lord came to bind up the broken-hearted. If you examine his version of the text, you will read that the Lord came to *cure* them.[21] That is going still further, because you may bind a wound up and yet fail to cure it; but Jesus never fails in His surgery. He whose own heart was broken knows how to cure broken hearts.

I have heard of people dying of a broken heart, but I always bless God when I meet with those who live with a broken heart, because it is written, "A broken and a contrite heart, O God, thou wilt not despise."[22] If you have that broken heart within you, beloved, Christ came to cure you; and He will do it, for He never came in vain: "He shall not fail nor be discouraged."[23] With sovereign power anointed from on high, He watches for the worst cases. Heart disease, incurable by man, is His specialty! His gospel touches the root of the soul's ill, the mischief that dwells in that place from where the issues of life flow. With pity, wisdom, power, and condescension, He bends over our broken bones; and before He is finished, He makes them all rejoice and sing glory to His name.

The second objective of His preaching is to proclaim *liberty to the captives*. Who are they? Captives were often persons taken in war and driven far away from home, as the Jews were in Babylon, where they wept, but could not sing. You that feel as if you were far off from God, far off from hope, far off even from fellowship with the Lord's people, you are the captives meant here—carried away against your will into the far off land of sin.

Captives in their captivity were generally treated as slaves, and compelled to work very hard without wages. Perhaps that is your condition; you have been working for the flesh and its lusts, working for the devil, working to please men and to gratify your own pride; and you have had no better reward than the poor prodigal that was not even put upon board wages, but left to starve and envy the greedy swine.

O, sin is a bad master, and its wages are worse than nothing. You have spent your money for that which is not bread, and your labor for that which does not satisfy. You have toiled in drudgery until your soul is brought down with labor, and you fall down and there is none to help.

Is that your case? Then the Lord Jesus is still the anointed of God to proclaim liberty to you. Behold, He will bring you back from banishment and bondage if you trust Him.

Are you one who is unable to do what you want to do? That is precisely the condition of a captive: he is in another's power and is not free to do his own will. You find sometimes that the will to do what is good is present with you, but you cannot find out how to do it. You are in bondage, brought into captivity to the law of sin and death.

You will think me cruel when I say that I am glad of it, yet I mean what I say, for it is for you captives, you far-away ones, you bond-slaves, you that cannot do the good that you want to do, that the Spirit of God rests upon Jesus on purpose that He may proclaim liberty to you.

There is an allusion here to the jubilee. The moment when the silver trumpet sounded in the morning because the fiftieth year had come, every person who was a captive throughout Judea's land was free, and none could hold him in bondage. They began to sing—

> The year of jubilee is come,
> Return, ye ransom'd captives, home.[24]

That is the song I want my hearers and readers to sing even now. Jesus Christ proclaims it—*proclaims it.* Do you notice that? A proclamation is a message to which all loyal subjects are sure to pay attention. In this case it is headed, not with V.R., *Vivat Regina!*[25] but *Vivat Rex Jehovah!* Long live Jehovah the King! He issues a proclamation from His throne; He bids His Son tell poor captive souls that Christ Jesus sets them free. Let them only believe Him, and they shall rise to instant liberty. May the Lord grant that many may accept this good news. We may expect it, for the Spirit of God rests upon the preaching of Christ.

Now, according to Isaiah, our Lord came for a third objective—*the opening of the prison to those that are bound.* Kindly look at Luke and see how that evangelist words it: he puts it thus—"And recovering of sight to the blind, to set at liberty them that are bruised." They say that everything loses by translation except a bishop; but here is a passage in which a text has greatly gained by translation; for, behold, it has doubly budded, and the one sentence is turned into two, and of the two each one is most precious.

Nor is the Greek translation, quoted in Luke, incorrect, for there is a wealth of meaning in the original Hebrew, which runs thus—"to the bound open opening," and this includes both the eyes and the prison. A blind man is, for all practical purposes, in prison. He is like a man shut up in a dark dungeon; his blindness is to him his cell, his fetter, and his closed door.

Isaiah in our text promises an opening of eyes, and so of prison doors; it is a complete opening, a glorious liberation from darkness within and without. Who could bring this to us but a divine Messiah? You, who are blind and bruised, hearken to this! Let Bartimaeus hear that Jesus of Nazareth passes by, and bids us bring the blind to Him.

You that see no light must not think that there is none, for the Sun of Righteousness has arisen; but, alas, you cannot see Him, and so the gospel day is as midnight to your sightless eyeballs. You pine as in a dreary dungeon, which you carry about with you; it is the atmosphere of unbelief, the dense fog of ignorance and fear. It all arises from your blind eyes; if these were opened, even the night would be light around you.

A blind man is the figure of one who cannot understand. You have heard the gospel hundreds of times, but you cannot grasp it; it remains a mystery to you. It has been put very plainly to you by minister, parent, teacher, and friend; you have read it in many simple books, but you have not found out its meaning yet. It is plain as the sun in the heavens, but you cannot see it.

We may make a thing very clear, but a blind man cannot see it, and such is your case: but behold the Lord Jesus Christ has come on purpose to open your eyes. Do you know that you are blind? Then you have begun to see already. He who sensibly mourns that he is blind has some portion of sight. If you already feel the darkness of sin in which you are groping, and are beginning to cry, "Lord, open my eyes," behold, Jesus Christ stands before you, and says, "The Lord has anointed me to give recovery of sight to the blind."

Believe in the Messenger of the covenant and He will touch those eyes of yours, and light shall stream into your soul. He will do for you what He did for the man who was born blind, and you shall be a wonder unto many.

I think I hear you say, "I understand it all now. Why didn't I see it before?" You shall never be blind again, for when the Lord opens the eyes of a man Satan himself cannot shut them. The divine oculist does His work for eternity.

The last sentence, according to Luke, is—*to set at liberty them that are bruised.* This is an extreme case of sorrow where a man is entirely under bondage, as, for instance, bondage through fear of death, or bondage under an awful sense of the law of God—bondage under doubt, and an apparent inability to believe anything; bondage under heavy apprehensions of approaching judgment; bondage under the idea that you are forsaken of God, and that your conscience is seared; bondage under the notion of your having committed the unpardonable sin.

And not only in bondage, but *bruised*; the fetters having hurt the limbs they bind, till the iron enters into the soul. You are suffering great spiritual pain, and it continues upon you from day to day. The chastisements of God leave bruises on your heart; you are so suffering that you write bitter things against yourself, and conclude that the bruises mean death.

Ah, poor bruised heart, there seems neither hope nor help for you; but it is not so, for according to the text Jesus Christ was anointed to set you at liberty. O, how happy you shall be if at this moment you can but trust the great Emancipator. Believe that if God anointed Him to do it He can set even you at liberty, though you lie in the inner prison of despair with your feet bruised by the stocks of doubt.

You who have been in bondage for years, you who have not dared to hope ever since you were a child, you who have given all up, you who consider yourselves to be already condemned, you who lie at death's dark door and seem already to feel the horrors of the bottomless pit—you most sad, most wretched of all mankind, daughters of sorrow, sisters of misery—even to you, specifically, is the gospel sent. While it is to be preached to every creature under heaven, it is especially to be proclaimed to you.

Here is comfort for all that mourn; for, behold, Jesus has come to proclaim liberty to such as you are, and to set free the bruised ones. I feel an inward happiness at having such a gospel to preach, and my only sad thought is that so many will refuse it. But, then, I am cheered with this—"The Lord knoweth them that are his."[26]

Those who are His sheep will hear His voice, and if you do not believe, it will prove that you are not of His sheep. All that the Father giveth to Him shall come to Him. The Lord says, "and him that cometh to me I will in no wise cast out."[27] May the Lord appear very graciously unto you, for Christ's sake. Amen.

CHAPTER 2

The Proclamation of Acceptance and Vengeance

To proclaim the acceptable year of the LORD, and the day of vengeance of our God; to comfort all that mourn...
—*Isaiah 61:2*

We have already stated that this Scripture speaks concerning the Lord Jesus Christ. We do not say this as if we relied upon our own opinion; for, as we noted in the previous sermon, we are assured of it by our Lord's own lips—since, reading this passage in the synagogue at Nazareth, He said, "This day is this scripture fulfilled in your ears."[1]

It is Jesus of Nazareth whom the Lord has anointed to preach deliverance to the captives and recovering of sight to the blind, and He has also come to make a proclamation that ushers in the year of acceptance and the day of vengeance.

Notice well the expression, *to proclaim*, because a proclamation is the message of a king, and where the word of a king is, there is power. The Lord Jesus Christ came into the world to announce the will of the King of kings. He says, "I am come in my Father's name,"[2] and again, "My doctrine is not mine, but his that sent me."[3]

Every word of the gospel is backed by the authority of "the King eternal, immortal, invisible,"[4] and he who rejects it is guilty of treason against Jehovah, God of all. The gospel is not of the nature of a commonplace invitation or human exhortation, which may be accepted or refused at will without involving guilt. No, the gospel is a divine proclamation, issued from the throne of the Eternal, which none can reject without becoming thereby rebels against the Infinite Majesty.

Now, if it be so, let us give the divine edict our most earnest attention, and take to our hearts what we hear. When a proclamation is issued by a head of state, all good citizens gather around to read what has been said to them, and to know what the supreme law may be: and so, when God proclaims His will, all right-hearted men desire to know what it is, and what bearing it has upon them, what the Lord demands or what the Lord promises, and what is their share therein. Listening to the gospel, then, should always be very solemn work, since it is listening to the word of God. Though the voice is that of man, yet the truth is of God; I pray you, never trifle with it.

Nor let it be forgotten that a proclamation must be treated with profound respect, not merely by receiving attention to its contents, but by gaining obedience to its demands. God does not speak to us by His Son so that we may be gratified by hearing the sound of His voice, but so that we may yield to His will. We are not to be hearers only, but doers of the word.

We should be quick in obedience to the command of the proclamation, swift in acceptance of its promise, and cheerful in submission to its demand. Who shall resist the proclamations of Jehovah? Is He not our Creator and King? Who is stubborn enough to refuse obedience? Or who is so defiant as to debate His authority?

Shall not He who made heaven and earth, and shakes them when He pleases, and will destroy them at His pleasure, be regarded with reverential awe by the creatures of His hand? O, Son of God, since it is a divine proclamation which You publish, send forth Your Holy Spirit that we may receive it with deepest reverence and lowliest obedience, lest, through our neglect, we show contempt toward You as well as to Your Father.

When a proclamation is not made by an ordinary herald, but when the Prince Himself comes forth to declare His Father's will, then all hearts should be moved to sevenfold attention. It is the Son of God, anointed by the Spirit of God, who acts as herald unto us, and so by each Person of the divine Trinity we are called upon to bow a listening ear and an obedient heart to what the Lord proclaims.

Attention, then! The Messenger of the Covenant makes proclamation! Attention for the King of kings!

With this as a preface, let me point out that there are three parts in the proclamation worthy of our best attention: the first is *the acceptable year,* the next, *the vengeance day,* and the third, *the comfort derived from both*—"to comfort all that mourn."

I. Jesus, in the first place, proclaims THE ACCEPTABLE YEAR OF THE LORD. Carefully examine this expression, and it comes to this—the year of the Lord and the year of acceptance.

Now, what was the *year of the Lord?* There can be, I think, very little question that this relates to the jubilee year. Every seventh year was the Lord's year, and it was to be a Sabbath of rest to the land; but the seventh seventh year, the fiftieth year, which the Lord reserved unto Himself, was the year of the Lord in a very marked and special sense.

Now, our Lord Jesus has come to proclaim a period of jubilee to the true seed of Israel. The seed of Abraham now are not the seed according to the law, but are those born after the promise. There are privileges reserved for Israel after the flesh, which they will yet receive in the day when they shall acknowledge Christ to be the Messiah. Yet every great blessing which was promised to Abraham's seed after the flesh is now virtually promised to Israel after the Spirit, to those who by faith are the children of believing Abraham.

Now, beloved, to all who believe, our Lord Jesus proclaims a year of jubilee. Let us dwell upon the four privileges of the jubilee, and accept with delight the proclamation that our Lord has made.

In the year of jubilee, as we read in the twenty-fifth chapter of Leviticus, there was *a release of all persons* who had sold themselves for servants. Pinched by great poverty, and unable to meet their debts, it sometimes happened that men were compelled to say to their creditor, "Take us and our wives and children, and accept our services instead of money. We have no goods or chattels, and our land has been mortgaged long ago. But we are here; we cannot pay in any other way—give us food and raiment and lodging, and we will put ourselves under apprenticeship to you."

The Law of Moses ordained that such persons were not to be treated harshly, nor regarded as slaves, but as hired servants. Still, it must have been an unpleasant condition of servitude for a freeborn Israelite. How happy then was the morning when the jubilee trumpet sounded, and the generous law came into operation that said, "He shall serve thee unto the year of jubilee, but then shall he depart from thee, both he and his children with him."[5]

From that moment, he owed no more service, however great his debt might have been. He looked upon his wife and children and rejoiced that they were all his own and all free from the yoke—they could therefore return at once to the possession of their fathers, all live in the cottage in which they formerly dwelt, and enjoy the piece of land which they had formerly called their own.

Liberty—that joy-filled sound—liberty had come to them. Now, it was of no importance that they had long been under obligations to the creditor, for those obligations ceased on the sound of the sacred trumpet. Beloved friend, proclamation is made to you in the Lord's name that if you are under bondage to sin and to sinful habits, there is liberty for you: faith in Jesus will set you free.

If you are in bondage under justice and the broken law, there is deliverance, for Jesus has borne the penalty due for transgression. If you are under bondage through fear of death, or from the rage of Satan, our divine Lord and Master has come into the world on purpose to break those bonds. You need be bound no longer; if you believe in Jesus you *are* bound no longer; but you are set free from the servitude of the law, from the slavery of Satan and from the dread of death.

Take the liberty that the great Lord freely presents to you, and be no longer a slave. Jesus has finished atonement, and brought in redemption, and believers are free. Accept, I beseech you, His full emancipation, and rejoice therein.

The next jubilee blessing was *the redemption of alienated possessions.* Every man had his own plot of ground in the Holy Land, but through the pressure of the times it sometimes happened that a man alienated his property: he was in need of ready money, his children wanted bread to eat, and he, therefore, parted with his land. It was gone: the vines and the fig trees, the corn and the oil, had passed over to another; but it was not gone forever, for he had no power to sell it for a period of time beyond the year of jubilee.

Thereby, when the joyful morning dawned, he went back to his family estate; it was all his own again, clear of all encumbrances. The little homestead, and the farmyard, and the fields, and the garden—all had come back to him, and no one could dispute his right.

Just so, my Lord and Master declares to all who believe in Him that the estate that Adam forfeited is restored to all for whom the Second Adam died. The alienated heritage is ours again. The great Father's love, and favor, and care—yes, all things, whether things present or things to come, or life or death—all are ours, and we are Christ's and Christ is God's.

If we are believers, and are of the true seed of Israel, this day the Lord Jesus proclaims to us a restoration of all the lost privileges and blessings that originally belonged to manhood. Behold, believer, all covenant mercies are yours;

rejoice in them! Partake of heavenly blessings freely. Let your soul rejoice in its portion, and delight itself in fullness.

It followed, also, as a third blessing of the year of the Lord that *all debts were discharged.* The man who had sold himself had, as it were, consolidated his debts by selling himself. This implied a full and final discharge at the jubilee. The person also who had mortgaged his land up to the jubilee year had discharged his debts thereby, and when the man received back himself and his property, no further liability rested upon him. He was cleared of all charges.

The jubilee did not give the man back himself and his land under a reserve, but without reserve. If debt had still been owed, the release would have been a mere farce, since he would have had to mortgage his land and sell himself again directly to meet the demand. No, there was a full discharge, a canceling of all debts, a removal of all encumbrances upon the man and upon his estate, and he was free.

What a joy this must have been! He who is in debt is in danger; an honest man sleeps on a hard bed till he has paid what he owes. He who is immersed in debt is plunged in misery, driven to his wits' end, not knowing what to do. Happy is he who has a discharge, full, free, and final, from all liabilities, once and for all.

Now behold, believer in Jesus, your innumerable liabilities are all met and ended; the handwriting that was against you is taken away and nailed to the cross, receipted in crimson lines by Jesus' precious blood. Being justified by faith you are clear before the sight of the Eternal; no one can place anything to your charge. What joyful notes are these! Jesus makes the proclamation. Who will not believe it and be glad?

A fourth blessing of the jubilee trumpet was *rest.* They had their lands, but they were not to cultivate them for a year. No more the spade and the plough, the sickle and the flail—

they were to put away instruments of labor, and rest for twelve months. Think of a whole year of perfect rest, wherein they might worship and adore God all week, make every day a holy festival, and the whole year a Sabbath of Sabbaths unto the Most High.

The Israelites had large privileges under the ceremonial covenant, if they had lived up to it; but they failed to do so; for it has sometimes been questioned whether they ever kept a jubilee at all, and whether the Sabbatic[6] year was even once observed.

If they had obeyed the Lord they would have been favored indeed; for in the matter of holidays and quiet resting times they were favored above all people. Think of one year in seven of absolute cessation from toil. What peaceful rest for them!

And then they had also the year after the seventh seven, so that every man who reached the fiftieth year enjoyed two consecutive years of absolute rest from all labor, and yet knew no want, for the ground brought forth plentifully, and every man helped himself. Those having land had a good store to last them through three years, and the spontaneous produce of the soil fed those who had no land.

We do not live under such laws, and if we did I am afraid we should not have the faith to trust in the Lord and avail ourselves of the divinely appointed holiday. But, beloved, we rest spiritually. He that believes in the Lord Jesus Christ has entered into rest. Now he no longer strives to work out a righteousness of his own, for he has already a divine one. He needs no other. It is his pleasure to worship God, but he no longer trembles beneath His wrath; it is his delight to do His commandments, but he no longer toils and frets as a slave under the law; he has become a free man, and a beloved child, and the peace of God which passes all understanding keeps his heart and mind.

Being justified by faith he has peace with God, and enjoys the influences of the divine Comforter whose indwelling gives rest to the soul.

The jubilee year, according to the text, was called "*the year of the Lord*"; and the reason for all the four jubilee blessings was found in the Lord. First, the servants were set free because God said, "They are my servants, which I brought forth out of the land of Egypt...."[7]

Ah, poor burdened soul, if you believe in Christ you shall go free, for you are the Lord's own—His chosen, His redeemed, and therefore He claims you, and will allow no other lord to have dominion over you. The devil seeks to lay an embargo upon you, and hold you a slave, but Jesus says, "Let go of My captives, for I have redeemed them with My blood." Jesus claims you, O penitent soul; He cries to sin as once the Lord said to Pharaoh, "Thus saith the LORD, Let my people go...."[8] Jesus says of each repenting soul, "Loose him and let him go, for he is Mine. My Father gave him to Me—he is My chosen, My beloved. Neither sin nor Satan, nor death nor hell, shall hold him, for he is Mine."

The land also was set free for this same reason, for concerning it the Lord said, "The land is Mine."[9] The freehold of the land was vested in Jehovah Himself. Consequently, He ordained that no man should hold any portion of it by right of purchase beyond the fiftieth year, for the land was entailed and at the Jubilee Year must go back to those for whom He had appointed it.

So the blessings of the everlasting covenant are God's, and therefore He appoints them unto you, poor believing sinner, and you shall have them, for the divine decree shall not be frustrated. As surely as He appointed Christ to reign, and placed Him on the throne, so does He appoint you to reign with Him, and you shall sit upon His throne though all the devils in hell should tell you it shall not be so.

So, too, the debts were all discharged, because on the day before the jubilee the great atonement had swept away all transgression and indebtedness towards God, and He would have His people forgive all the debts of their fellow men. All things are the Lord's, and He exercised His crown rights on the day of jubilee so far as to declare all debts discharged. "The earth is the LORD's, and the fullness thereof,"[10] was the motto of the jubilee, and sufficient reason for the canceling of obligations between man and man.

As for rest, that came also, because it was God's year, holy unto the Lord. "A jubilee shall that fiftieth year be unto you: ye shall not sow, neither reap that which groweth of itself in it, nor gather *the grapes* in it of thy vine undressed. For it *is* the jubilee; it shall be holy unto you: ye shall eat the increase thereof out of the field."[11]

During man's years the earth brings forth thorns and thistles, and man must earn his bread with the sweat of his face; but when God's year comes, then the wilderness and the solitary place are glad, and the desert rejoices and blossoms as the rose. When the Lord's own kingdom comes, then shall the earth yield her increase, as she has never done before.

Dear friend, I trust you know the blessedness of living in God's year, for you live by faith upon His providence, casting all your care upon Him, for He cares for you. This is the Sabbath of the soul, the counterpart of heaven.

You behold the work of atonement fully accomplished on your behalf, and know yourself to be delivered from all servitude under the law, and therefore your heart leaps within you. You are completely delivered, set free, washed in the blood of the Lamb, and therefore you come to Zion with songs and everlasting joy upon your head.

But the text speaks also of the *acceptable year of the Lord.* Now, our Lord Jesus Christ has come to proclaim to sinners the Lord's acceptance of guilty men through His great sacrifice. Apart from the work of our Lord Jesus, men as sinners are unacceptable to God. Perhaps you are just now experiencing the misery of being in that condition and the horror of conviction that the Lord is weary of you and your vain oblations.

Since you have come in your own name and righteousness, God has not accepted you. Neither has He heard your prayers nor listened to your cries, nor had respect unto your religious observances, for He says, "Even though you make many prayers, I will not hear."[12]

If the Spirit of God has convinced you of your natural unacceptability with God, you must have been brought into a very sad state indeed; for not to be accepted of God, and to be aware of it, is cause for intense sorrow. But now be assured, if you believe in Jesus, that you are accepted of God. Regardless of your infirmities and sins you are "accepted in the Beloved," by Him who has said, "I will accept you with your sweet savor."[13]

And now, since you are thus accepted, your petitions shall come up with acceptance before the Lord. As for your prayers, God hears them; as for your tears, He puts them into His bottle; as for your works, He counts them to be fruits of His Spirit and accepts them. Yes, now that you are accepted in Christ, all that you are and all that you have, and all you do—the whole of you—is well pleasing to God through Jesus Christ our Lord.

I am happy many times over to have such a subject as this. Are you willing now to believe in Jesus? I tell you this is the acceptable year of the Lord; God is reconciled, man is favored, blessings abound. Now is the accepted time, now is the day of salvation. Let sin be confessed and the confession shall be accepted, and you shall find forgiveness. Let transgression be repented of, the repentance shall be accepted, and you shall hear a voice saying, "Go, and sin no more; your sins, which are many, are forgiven you."

Greetings to you that are graciously accepted: you are blessed among women! And you too, my brother! Remember the words of Solomon, "Go thy way, eat thy bread with joy, and drink thy wine with a merry heart; for God now accepteth thy works."[14]

Come to Jesus by faith, for though you come with a limping walk, and your faith is feeble, yet shall you be accepted. Come you who have a broken heart and a sorrowing spirit, you who are downcast and dare not look up: this is no common time. The Lord Jesus has made it a red-letter year for you, for He proclaims a year of grace and acceptance.

Behold in this *anno Domini*, or year of our Lord, we have a choice year of grace set apart for us. Who will not come to our gracious Prince, accept His mercy, and live?

Thus you see we get a double meaning from the text— the Year of Jubilee with all its accumulated privileges of free grace, and the year of acceptance in which whosoever will may come, and God will accept him if he comes in the name of Jesus, trusting only in the atoning blood.

II. May the Lord help us while we ponder the second part of the text: THE DAY OF VENGEANCE OF OUR GOD. Does not the sound of vengeance grate upon your ear? Does it not seem discordant to the sweet tone of the passage? Vengeance! Shall that happen side by side with acceptance?

Yes, beloved, this is the mystery of the gospel: the system of redemption marries justice and mercy; the method of certainty unites severity and grace; the economy of substitution blends acceptance and vengeance. This gospel mystery is to be proclaimed to every creature under heaven, for it is the power of God unto salvation to every one that believes.

See, in the text you have the heart of God laid bare, for you have the year of acceptance coupled with the day of vengeance. Well and very sweetly has Dr. Watts[15] expressed it thusly—

Here I behold His inmost heart,
Where grace and vengeance strangely join,
Piercing His Son with sharpest smart,
To make the purchased pleasure mine.

Let us explain this strange blending, and at the same time expound the text.

In the first place, whenever there is a day of mercy to those who believe, it is always a day of responsibility to those who reject it. And if they continue in that state, it is a day of increased wrath to unbelievers. It is not possible for the gospel to be without some effect. If it be a characteristic flavor of life unto life to those who receive it, it must of necessity from its own intrinsic vigor be an aroma of death unto death to those who reject it.

To this sword there are two edges—one will kill our fears, or the other will surely kill our pride and destroy our vain hopes if we do not yield to Christ. When our Lord read this passage at Nazareth, He stopped short; He did not read it all. He read as far down as "to proclaim the acceptable year of the Lord," and then He closed the book and gave it to the minister and sat down.

I suppose that at the beginning of His ministry, before He had been rejected by the nation and before He had suffered for sin, He wisely chose to allude to the gentler topics rather than to the more stern and terrible ones. But He did not conclude His ministry without referring to the stern words that followed those that He had read. If you will turn to Luke's twenty-first chapter you will find Him saying—

> Then let them which are in Judea flee to the mountains; and let them which are in the midst of it depart out; and let not them that are in the countries enter thereinto. For these be the days of vengeance, that all things which are written may be fulfilled.[16]

You know the story of the siege of Jerusalem, the most harrowing of all narratives, for the anger of God was concentrated upon that wicked city beyond all precedent. Because they rejected Christ, vengeance came upon them. They filled up the measure of their iniquity when at last they disowned their King and cried out, "Away with Him, away with Him, let Him be crucified."[17]

Be aware then, dear friend, that if you have heard the gospel and rejected it, you have incurred great guilt, and you can never sin so cheaply as you did before; for you there will be a day of vengeance above the men of Sodom and Gomorrah, because you have perpetrated a crime which they were not capable of committing—you have rejected the Christ of God. The year of acceptance to believers will be a day of vengeance to those who do not obey His gospel.

Another meaning of the text comes out in the fact that *there is appointed a day of vengeance for all the enemies of Christ,* and this will happen in that bright future day for which we are looking. Not merely for rejecters of His gospel will there be vengeance, but for all men and fallen spirits who dare to oppose His government, His authority, and rule.

Behold, He comes a second time; every winged hour hastens His advent, and when He comes it will be a great and a dreadful day to His foes. It will be to His saints the day of their revelation, manifestation, and acceptance, but to the ungodly "the day of vengeance of our God."[18] Enoch, the seventh from Adam, prophesied of these, saying, "Behold, the Lord comes with ten thousands of his saints, to execute judgment upon all, and to convince all that are ungodly among them of all their ungodly deeds which they have ungodly committed, and of all their hard *speeches* which ungodly sinners have spoken against him."[19]

Paul also bears witness that the Lord Jesus shall be revealed from heaven with His mighty angels, "in flaming fire taking vengeance on them that know not God, and that obey not the gospel of our Lord Jesus Christ: who shall be punished with everlasting destruction from the presence of the Lord, and from the glory of his power; when he shall come to be glorified in his saints, and to be admired in all them that believe."[20] Note the vengeance and the grace combined.

The prophet Isaiah saw our great Champion returning from His last fight, and thus spoke concerning Him:

Who is this who comes from Edom, with dyed garments from Bozrah? this *that is* glorious in his apparel, traveling

in the greatness of his strength? I that speak in righteousness, mighty to save.

Wherefore *art thou* red in thine apparel, and thy
garments like him that treadeth in the winevat?

I have trodden the winepress alone; and of the people
there was none with me: for I will tread them in mine anger,
and trample them in my fury, and their blood shall be
sprinkled upon my garments, and I will stain all my
raiment.

For the day of vengeance is in mine heart, and the year
of my redeemed is come.[21]

Note the connection between the day of vengeance and
the year of the redeemed. At the Second Advent, Christ will
come to be glorified in His saints, and they shall be
manifested in the fullness of their acceptance; but it will be
an overwhelming day of vengeance for all those who have
hardened their hearts and continued in their sins:

For, behold, the day cometh, that shall burn as an oven;
and all the proud, yea, and all that do wickedly, shall be
stubble: and the day that cometh shall burn them up, saith
the LORD of hosts, that it shall leave them neither root nor
branch.[22]

However, I consider that the chief meaning of the text
lies in this—that "the day of vengeance of our God" was that
day when He made all the transgressions of His people to
meet upon the head of our great Surety.[23] Sin with many
streams had been flowing down the hills of time and forming
by their dread accumulation one vast and fathomless lake.
Into this the sinner's Substitute must be plunged. He had a
baptism to be baptized with and He must endure it, or all
His chosen must perish forever. That was a day of vengeance
when all the waves and billows of divine wrath went over His
innocent head.

Came at length the dreadful night;
    Vengeance with its iron rod
Stood, and with collected might
    Bruised the harmless Lamb of God.

> See, my soul, thy Savior see,
> Prostrate in Gethsemane!

From His blessed person there distilled a bloody sweat, for His soul was exceedingly sorrowful even unto death. All through the night, with scourgings and buffetings and spittings of cruel men, He was tortured and abused; He was rejected, despised, maltreated, and pierced in His inmost soul by man's scorn and cruelty; then in the morning He was taken out to be crucified, for nothing could suffice short of His death.

The outward sorrows of crucifixion may be known, but the inward griefs we cannot know, for what our Lord endured was beyond what any mortal man could have borne. The infinity of the Godhead aided the manhood, and I believe that Hart was right in saying He

> Bore all Incarnate God could bear
> With strength enough, but none to spare.[24]

It was an awful "day of vengeance of our God," for the voice cried aloud, "Awake, O sword, against my shepherd, and against the man *that is* my fellow, saith the LORD of hosts...."[25]

The doctrine that justice was executed upon our great Substitute is the most important that was ever propounded in the hearing of men; it is the sum and substance of the whole gospel, and I fear that the church which rejects it is no longer a church of Christ. Substitution is as much a standing or falling article in the church as the doctrine of justification by faith itself. Beloved, there would never have been an acceptable year if there had not been a day of vengeance. You can be sure of this.

And now let us look at the instructive type by which this truth was taught to Israel of old. The year of jubilee began with the Day of Atonement. "Then shalt thou cause the trumpet of the jubilee to sound on the tenth *day* of the seventh month, in the day of atonement shall ye make the trumpet sound throughout all your land."[26]

What did the high priest do on that day? Read the seventeenth chapter of Leviticus. On that day, he washed himself and came forth before the people, wearing neither his breastplate, nor his garments of glory and beauty, blue and scarlet and fine linen; but the high priest wore the ordinary linen garments of a common priest. Even thus the Lord, who counted it not robbery to be equal with God, laid aside all His glory, and was found in fashion as a man.

Then the priest took a bullock, and, having offered it, went within the veil with the censer full of burning coals of fire, and sweet incense beaten small, with which he filled the inner court with perfumed smoke. After this he took the blood of the bullock and sprinkled it before the mercy seat seven times. Thus our Lord entered within the veil with His own blood and with the sweet incense of His own merits, to make atonement for us.

Of the two goats, one was killed as a sin offering, and his blood was sprinkled within the veil, and the other was used for a scapegoat. Upon the head of the scapegoat Aaron laid both his hands, and confessed all the iniquities of the children of Israel, "putting them upon the head of the goat,"[27] which was then taken into the wilderness, representing the carrying away of sin into oblivion.

Do you not see your Lord and Master bearing your sin away? "As far as the east is from the west, *so* far hath he removed our transgressions from us."[28]

Is there any wonder that a jubilee of peace should follow such a taking away of iniquity as our great High Priest has accomplished? Jesus has entered into the heavens for us; can we doubt that we are, through Him, accepted by God?

The bodies of the beasts whose blood was brought into the sanctuary for sin on the day of atonement were not allowed to remain in the holy place, but were carried outside the camp to be utterly consumed with fire, in token that sin is loathsome in the sight of God, and must be put away from His presence. In this way our Lord suffered outside the gates of Jerusalem and cried, "My God, my God, why hast thou forsaken me?"[29] "For Christ also hath suffered once for sins, the just for the unjust, that he might bring us to God...."[30] All this was absolutely necessary to a jubilee.

Without atonement, there is no rejoicing. Before there can be acceptance for a single sinner, sin must be laid on Jesus and carried away. The blood of Jesus must be shed, and must be presented within the veil, for "without shedding of blood there is no remission"[31] of sin. No man living under heaven can have pardon or acceptance with God in any way but by the bloody sacrifice which our Redeemer offered when He bowed His head and gave up His spirit, in His last breath, on Calvary.

This great truth we must never obscure, nor cease to proclaim as long as we have a tongue for speech. The day of vengeance, then, is intimately connected with the year of acceptance. Notice, beloved one, *they must be so connected experimentally in the heart of all God's people by the teaching of the Holy Spirit*, for whenever Christ comes to make us live, the law comes first to kill us. There is no healing without previous wounding. Depend upon it; there never will be a sense of acceptance in any man until first he has had a sense of the just and righteous vengeance of God against his sin.

Have you noticed that remarkable parallel to our text in Isaiah chapter thirty-five, where salvation and vengeance are so closely joined? There we read:

> Strengthen ye the weak hands, and confirm the feeble knees.
>
> Say to them *that are* of a fearful heart, Be strong, fear not: behold, your God will come *with* vengeance, *even* God with a recompense; he will come and save you.
>
> Then the eyes of the blind shall be opened, and the ears of the deaf shall be unstopped.
>
> Then shall the lame *man* leap as an hart, and the tongue of the dumb sing: for in the wilderness shall waters break out, and streams in the desert.[32]

O, poor, trembling, convinced sinner, God has come with vengeance to you, but His intent is to save you. Every soul that is saved must feel that wrath is deserved and that the death-punishment is due on account of sin; when this is known and felt, acceptance by faith will follow. There must be a death blow struck at all self-sufficiency and self-righteousness, and the man must be laid as dead at the feet of Christ before ever he will look up and find life and healing in the great atoning sacrifice.

When our Lord puts on the helmet of salvation, He also girds about Him the garments of vengeance, and we must see Him in all His array.[33] The day of vengeance is a necessary companion to the year of acceptance. Have they gone together in your experience?

III. The last point we propose to consider is THE COMFORT FOR MOURNERS DERIVABLE FROM BOTH THESE THINGS. *To comfort all that mourn.*

Now, I have no hope of interesting you, much less of doing you any good, my dear reader, if you do not come under the description of a mourner. The sower's duty is to sow the seed everywhere, but he knows within himself that it will not take root anywhere except where the plough has been first at work.

If the Lord has made you a mourner, then this blessed subject will comfort you; but the Lord never comforts those who do not want comfort. If you can save yourself, go and do it: if you are righteous, "...he that is righteous, let him be righteous still...."[34]

I say it in sarcasm, as you perceive, for you cannot save yourself, nor are you righteous; but if you think so, go your way and try it—vainly try it, for surely when you have fanned your best works into a flame, and have walked by the light of the sparks of the fire which you have kindled, you shall have this at the Lord's hands—you shall lie down in sorrow and be astonished that you were ever so mad as to dream of self-salvation or of justification by your own works.

But O, poor mourner, what joy is here, joy because this is the year of acceptance, and in the year of acceptance, or jubilee, men were set free and their lands were restored without money. No man ever paid a penny of redemption money on the jubilee morning: every man was free *simply because jubilee was proclaimed.* No merit was demanded, no protest was offered, no delay allowed, no dispute permitted. Jubilee came, and the bondman was free.

And now, today, whosoever believes in Jesus is saved, pardoned, freed—without money having been paid, without merit, without preparation, simply because he believes, and God declares that he that believes is justified from all things from which he could not be justified by the Law of Moses.

Do you believe? Then you are of the house of Israel, and you have God's guarantee for it—you are free. Rejoice in your liberty! Surely this is sweet comfort for all that mourn. Do not look for any marks and evidences, signs and tokens; do not look for any of your own merits or attainments; do not look for any progress in grace or advancement in piety as a ground of salvation; listen only to the proclamation of the gospel, and accept the divine decree that ordains a jubilee.

Are you of the chosen seed? Do you believe in Jesus? Then for you it is an accepted year. Come, bring your griefs and sorrows, and leave them at the cross, for the Lord accepts you, and who shall tell you otherwise?

An equal joy-note, however, rings out from the other sentence concerning the day of vengeance. If the day of vengeance took place when our Lord died, then it is over. The day of vengeance was past and gone eighteen hundred years ago and more.

> Now no more His wrath we dread,
> Vengeance smote our Surety's head;
> Legal claims are fully met,
> Jesus paid the dreadful debt.

Beloved, do you bleed for sin and mourn because of it? It may be so; but it has ceased to be, for Christ made an end of it when He took it up to His cross and bore it there in His own body on the tree.

O, believer, are you bowed down and troubled on account of past sin? It is right you should repent, yet remember your past sin exists no more. It is cancelled, for the day of vengeance is over.

God will not take vengeance twice for the same sin. Either the atonement that Jesus offered was enough, or it was not. If it was not, then what sorrow and woe for us, for we shall die. But if it was sufficient—if "It is finished!"[35] was not a lie but a truth—then He has "finished transgression and made an end of sin."[36] The sin of the believer is annihilated and abolished, and can never be laid to his charge. Let us rejoice that the day of vengeance is over, and the year of acceptance has begun.

In another sense, however, it may be that some are mourning because of the temptations of Satan. Here, too, they may be comforted, for Jesus has come to take vengeance on the evil one, and the God of peace shall bruise Satan under your feet shortly. Are you afraid of death? Behold Christ has taken revenge on death, for He bids you cry, because of His resurrection, "O death, where *is* thy sting? O grave, where *is* thy victory?"[37]

Are we mourning today because our dear ones are not converted? It is a good thing to mourn on that account, but let us take comfort, for this is an acceptable year; let us pray for them, and the Lord will save them.

Are we mourning because sin is rampant in the wide world? Let us rejoice, for our Lord has broken the dragon's head, and the day of vengeance must come when the Lord will overthrow the powers of darkness.

Have we been looking with mournful spirit upon old Rome, and the Mohammedan imposture, and the power of Buddhism and Brahminism, and the sway of other ancient idolatries? Let us be glad. Behold the Avenger cometh! He comes a second time, and comes conquering and to conquer.

Then shall the day of His vengeance be in His heart, and the year of His redeemed shall come.

The deceiver shall be torn, no more to curse the sons of men with his pretensions to be the victor of God. In blackest night shall set forever the crescent of Mohammed, which already wanes. Its baleful light shall no more afflict unhappy nations. Then, by the rod of iron that Jesus wields, the gods of the Hindus and Chinese shall fall, like potters' broken vessels.

At Jesus' appearing the whole earth shall acknowledge that He who was "despised and rejected by men"[38] is "King of kings and Lord of lords."[39] Behold, the day comes swiftly; let all that mourn be comforted. The day of vengeance, the full year of the millennial glory, the day of the overthrow of error, the year of the restoration of creation to all her former beauty, the age when God shall be all in all, is near at hand. Hasten it, O Lord. Amen.

CHAPTER 3

Gracious Appointments for Zion's Mourners

To appoint unto them that mourn in Zion...—*Isaiah 61:3*a

In the last discourse we dwelt upon the singular combination of vengeance and acceptance—"To proclaim the acceptable year of the LORD, and the day of vengeance of our God...." The necessary connection between the two was shown.

We next observed that because God has executed vengeance upon Christ, and has now accepted His people, there is reasonable ground of comfort for all that mourn. The Savior came "to comfort all that mourn,"[1] and His sacrifice is for them a full fountain of hope. No mourner need despond, much less despair, since God has executed the sentence of His wrath upon the Great Substitute, so that He might freely accept every sinner that believes.

We are now going a step farther, and instead of reminding you that those who mourn may be comforted, we shall proclaim the loving-kindness of the Lord, and make it clear that God has a special regard for mourners, and that He has appointed, provided, and reserved special blessings for them. So runs the eternal purpose. Our Lord declared this in the opening of His Sermon on the Mount: "Blessed *are* they that mourn: for they shall be comforted."[2]

The anointed Savior came "to appoint unto them that mourn in Zion." Consider carefully four things. *What are they doing?* They mourn. *Where are they doing it?* In Zion. *Who thinks of them?* The Great God who here speaks about them. And *what is He doing for them?* His purposes are "to appoint unto them that mourn in Zion."

I. First, then, WHAT ARE THEY DOING—these people of whom the text speaks? They are mourning. Not a very cheerful occupation. Nobody will be very much attracted towards them by that fact. Most choose lively, merry company, and mourners generally are left alone.

Are they not to be greatly pitied? Reason thinks so; but faith has heard Jesus say, "Blessed are they that mourn"; and, therefore, she believes it to be better to be a mourning saint than a merry sinner, and she is willing to take her place on the stool of penitence and weep, rather than sit in the seat of the scorner and laugh.

Because these persons mourn, *they differ from other people.* If they are mourning in Zion, their case is special. There is evidently a distinction between them and the great majority of humanity, for worldly people are often lighthearted, making merry and never thinking about or looking into the future. So unreal is their happiness that it would not bear the weight of an hour's quiet consideration, and so they laugh in order to drown all thought of their true situation.

They favor pastimes, amusements, and fun: these are for the lighthearted, carefree ones, who drink wine by the bowlful and "drive dull care away." It is greatly wise for a man to commune with his own heart in quiet solitude; but foolish ones never do this, and hence they emit a brief light with effervescent mirth, and they sparkle with false joy.

Those who mourn in Zion are very different from these excitable, superficial people; in fact, they cannot bear them, but are grieved with their foolish conversation, as any man of sense may well be. Who wants to have these flies forever buzzing about him?

The gracious ones who mourn in Zion are as different from them as the lily from the hemlock, or as the dove from the crow. He who allows reason to take its proper place, and to be taught right reason by the word of God, from that time separates himself from the staggering crowd and takes the cool sequestered path which leads to God.

Equally does this mourning separate the gospel mourner from the obstinate and the daring. For, sad to say, many are so wicked as to wear an insolent expression and exhibit a heart of steel in the presence of the Lord. They defy the divine wrath, and impudently scorn the punishment due to sin. Like Pharaoh, they ask, "Who *is* the LORD, that I should obey His voice...?"[3] They despise death, judgment, and eternity, and set themselves in battle array against the Almighty.

Those who mourn in Zion are not like this, for they tremble at the word of the Lord. Their hearts are sensitive to the faintest sign of God's displeasure, and when they know that they have done that which is grievous in His sight, immediately their sorrow overflows; they deeply lament their provocations, and humbly pray that they may be kept from further offenses.

Zion's mourners are also very different from the self-conceited who are puffed up with high notions of their own excellence. They are never known to assert that from their youth up they have kept all the commandments, nor do they even dream of thanking God that they are better than others. They find no room for boasting; rather, they abhor themselves in dust and ashes. Their sins, foolishness, and failings are a daily burden to them, and they loathe the very idea of self-satisfaction.

Those who mourn in Zion are not among those who loudly glory in the abundance of their grace and think that they are beyond the reach of temptation. You will never hear them cry, "My mountain stands firm: I shall never be moved"; but their prayer is, "Hold me up, and I shall be safe."

Holy anxiety to be found sincere and acceptable with God prevents all self-confidence. I would not encourage doubts and fears, but I will go the length of the poet, and say—

> He that never doubted of his state,
> He may—perhaps he may, too late.

I fear that many who dream that they possess strong faith are under a strong delusion to believe a lie. Instead of having the confidence that is wrought of the Spirit of God, which is quite consistent with holy mourning, they feel a false confidence based upon themselves, and therefore founded upon the sand. This puffs them up with a false peace, and makes them talk with extreme pride, to the sorrow of the Lord's wounded ones.

The Lord's people should prudently get out of the way of these lofty spirits, who grieve the humble in heart. They are the strong cattle, of which Ezekiel speaks,[4] which thrust with horn and shoulder, and despise the weak ones whom God has chosen.

Lord, let my portion be with the mourners, and not with the boasters. Let me take my share with those who weep for sin, and weep after You; and as for those who are careless, or those who are rebellious, or those who are self-righteous, let them take their frothy joy and drain the cup, for true saints do not desire its intoxicating draught.

The mourners in Zion are not only different from other people, but they are also *much changed from their former selves.* They are scarcely aware of the great change that they have undergone, but even their mourning is evidence that they are new creatures.

The things wherein they formerly rejoiced are now their horror, while other things they once despised they now eagerly desire. They have put away their ornaments: their finery of pride they have exchanged for the sackcloth of repentance; their noisy merriment for humble confession.

They now wonder how they could have thought the ways of sin to be pleasurable, and feel as if they could weep their eyes out, because of their extreme foolishness.

You would not think that they were the same people. In fact, to tell you the truth, they are not the same, for they have been born again, and have undergone a new creation, of which their humiliation before God is no cheap sign. Their hearts of stone have been taken away, and the Lord has given them hearts of flesh to feel, to tremble, to lament, and to seek the Lord.

God's mourners also find themselves *different from what they are at times even now;* for they see themselves wander, and immediately they quarrel with themselves, and show deep repentance daily.

The man who is satisfied with himself had better search his heart, for there are signs of rottenness about him. The man who is deeply discontented with himself is probably growing quickly into the full likeness of Christ.

Do you, dear friend, feel that you could justify yourself regarding all that you have done, or thought, or felt today from morning to evening—at home or abroad, in the shop or in the street? No, I am sure you will admit that in many things you have fallen short, and you will penitently grieve before the living God. You would not on any account do or say again all that you have done and said. You bless God who has sanctified you and delivered you from the dominion of sin; but still you have to express your suffering because sin has a fearful power to lead you into captivity.

Therefore, you are not pleased with yourself, and are more ready to join in a confession than in a hymn of self-glorifying. Of such mourners, the text says that God has appointed great things for them, and therefore let us pray the Holy Spirit to work in us this kind of mourning.

Now, *this mourning,* of which we are speaking, *is part and parcel of these people's lives.* When they began to live to Christ they began to mourn. Every child of God is born again with a tear in his eye. Dry-eyed faith is not the faith of God's elect. He who rejoices in Christ at the same time mourns for sin. Repentance is joined to faith by loving bands, as Siamese twins were united in one.

The new birth always takes place in the chamber of sorrow for sin; it cannot be otherwise. The true Christian was a mourner at conversion, and since then he has been a mourner, even in the happiest day he has known. When was that? The happiest day I ever knew was when I found Jesus to be my Savior, and when I felt the burden of my sin roll off me.

"O, happy day! When Jesus washed my sins away." But I mourned that day to think that I had been so greatly polluted, and had needed that my Lord should die to put away my sin. I mourned to think that I had not loved and trusted the Savior before; and before the sun went down I was mourning to think that I did not even then love my Lord as much as I desired.

I had not gone many paces on the road to heaven before I began to mourn that I limped so badly, that I traveled so slowly and was so little like my Lord. So, I know by experience that on the very brightest day of his spiritual experience a true believer still feels a soft, sweet mourning in his heart, falling like one of those gentle showers which cool the heat of our summer days and yield a pleasurable refreshment. Holy mourning is the blessed pillar of cloud that accompanies the redeemed of the Lord in their glad march to heaven.

Beloved, to some extent we live by mourning. Do not imagine we do not rejoice. Truly, we "rejoice with joy unspeakable and full of glory...."[5] This is quite consistent with holy mourning. We sorrow every day that there should be any remains of sin in us, that we should still be open to temptation, and should have the slightest inclination to evil.

We mourn that our eyes should look so longingly on vanity, and that our tongue should be so prone to speak unadvisedly. We mourn that our right hand should be so unskillful in holy service, and that we should so easily let others notice when we are giving to the Lord. We mourn especially that our heart should still be unbelieving, unfeeling, and fickle. Yes, we are very happy, but we mourn to think that, being so happy, we are not more holy; that, being so favored, we are not more consecrated. We "rejoice with trembling."

To the Lord's mourners, godly sorrow is so essentially a part of themselves that they grow *while they mourn*, and even grow by mourning. A man never becomes better until he is weary of being imperfect. He who is satisfied with his attainments will stay where he is; he who mourns that he is not yet up to the standard will press forward until he reaches it.

He that says, "My faith is weak," is the man who will become stronger in faith. He who confesses that his love is not as intense as it ought to be will have more love before long. He who mourns daily that he has not attained what he desires is by that very agony of spirit approaching the goal.

It will be well if mourning were our companion until we come to the gates of paradise, and there we shall mourn no longer. Yet, so precious is the mourning that the Spirit works in us that we might almost regret parting with it. Rowland Hill[6] used to say he felt half sorry to think that he must part with the tear of repentance at the gates of heaven; and he was right, for holy mourning is blessed, sweet, safe, and sanctifying. The bitterness is so completely evaporated that we can truly say,

> Lord, let me weep for nought but sin,
> And after none but Thee;
> And then I would—oh that I might!—
> A constant weeper be.

Dear friends, *holy mourning is no mere melancholy or sickly whim*; it has abundant reasons whereby to justify itself. We do not mourn because we give way to needless despondency; we lament because it would be utter madness to do otherwise: we cannot help mourning. A Christian grieves over himself and his shortcomings, and this not from mock-modesty, but because he sees so much to sigh over.

He will tell you that he never thinks worse of himself than he ought to do; that the very worst condemnation he has ever pronounced upon himself was most richly deserved. If you praise him, you pain him. If you commend him, he disowns your approval, and tells you that if you knew him better you would think less of him, and you would see so much infirmity and imperfection within him, that you would not again expose him to danger by uttering flatteries.

A child of God also mourns because he is in sympathy with others. It is one part of the work of grace in the soul to give us considerateness for our afflicted brothers and sisters in Christ. Is a child of God prosperous? He remembers others who are poor and in adversity, and he feels bound with them. He is a member of the body, and hence he suffers with the other members.

If each believer were distinct and separate, and kept his own joy to himself and his sorrow to himself, he might more often rejoice. However, being a member of a body that is always more or less afflicted, he weeps because others weep, and mourns because others mourn. The more sympathy you have in your nature the more sorrow you will experience. It is the unsympathetic man who laughs every day; but the friendly, tender, brotherly, Christ-like spirit must mourn. It is inevitable.

Mainly, believers mourn because of the sins of others. This great city furnishes us with abundant occasion for deep concern. You can hardly go down a street but you hear such filthy language that it makes your blood chill in your veins. The sharpest blow could not cause us more pain than the hearing of profanity. And then the Sabbath, how little is it regarded. The things of God, how little are they cared for! Everywhere a child of God with his eyes open must have them filled with tears, and if his heart be as it ought to be, it must be ready to break.

Sadly, the cause is frequently in the Christian's own family: he has an ungodly child or an unconverted wife. A Christian woman may have a drunken husband, or a godly daughter may have a dissipated father.

These things make life gloomy beyond expression. "Woe is me," cries the saint, "that I dwell as among lions, with those that are set on fire of hell." Unfavorable society makes a child of God sick at heart. As Lot was vexed with the filthy conversation of the wicked, and as David cried for the wings of a dove that he might fly away and be at rest, so do the saints pine in this world. Let such mourners take heart while they perceive in the text that Jesus has come to comfort all that mourn.

II. Now, secondly, let us note WHERE THESE PEOPLE ARE MOURNING. They are mourning *in Zion*. They could not carry their griefs to a better place. Sorrow is so common that we find mourners in Babylon, in Tyre, and even in Sodom and Gomorrah; but these are of a different order from the mourners in Zion.

If we are wearing our sackcloth in the house of the Lord, let us thank God, in the first place, that we are not mourning in hell. We might have been there. We should have been there if we had received our due. But, we are mourning where mourning meets with acceptance from God. We are lamenting where a dirge can be changed into a song.

I thank God also that we are not mourning like those who fiendishly regret that accidentally they have done some good thing. You remember how angry Pharaoh was with himself because he had let Israel go, and I have known men who have never been penitent until they have by mistake done something good, or given too much away. They could gnaw their own hearts out for having done a good turn to another. God save us from such diabolical mourning. Yet, it is not uncommon.

Also, we have known some who mourn, because they could not do others a mischief, because their hands were tied and they could not hurt God's people. Like Haman, they have fretted because of Mordecai.[7] They cannot endure the prosperity of the godly, but would gladly take advantage of them and turn them into the mire of the streets. That is a horrible mourning, which makes a man have fellowship with Satan.

Some even mourn because they cannot take a time of wild behavior in sin. They would like to indulge every vile passion, have a mint of money at their command, and no one to check them in any way. They mourn because they are hindered from destroying themselves. Such foolish ones mourn on the bar stool. They mourn in the synagogue of Satan. But, God's people mourn in Zion.

Now let us indulge ourselves with a visit to the courts of Zion to see where the mourners may be found. For from her outer walls even to her innermost courts, you will find her inhabited by them. Some of them mourn close to the walls of the holy city. Like the Jews of the present day, they have their wailing place under the walls of Jerusalem. Poor souls! They dare not enter into the holy place, and yet they will not, cannot go away.

They wait at the gates of wisdom's house and they delight in the posts of her doors. They never like to be away when the saints assemble, yet they feel as if they had no right to be there. They are satisfied with any corner, and are content to stand throughout the service. They take the lowest seats, and reverence the lowliest child of God.

They sometimes fear that the good word is not for them, and yet like the dogs they come under the table, hoping for a morsel. If it is a sermon full of thunder, "Yes, " they say, "the minister means me"; but if it is very sweet and full of comfort they say, "Alas, I dare not think that it is for me." They would not stay away from the holy congregation, for they feel that their only hope must lie in hearing the gospel, and they half hope that a word of comfort may be dropped for them; but they come trembling.

They are like the robin redbreast in winter. They venture near the house and tap upon the windowpane, and yet are half afraid to come in. When the cold is very severe and they are very hungry, they become daring, and pick up a crumb or two. Still, for the most part, they stand at the temple door and mourn. They are in Zion, and they sigh and cry because they feel unworthy so much as to lift their eyes towards heaven.

Well, the Lord appoints great blessings for you: He is good to those who seek Him. He hears the cry of the humble, and He will not despise their prayer. Now, if the arch-enemy should ever suggest to you that it is of no use for you to be found hearing the Word—for you have heard the preacher so many times, and even for years have remained unblessed, and therefore it is all hopeless—tell him he is a liar. Be all the more diligent in your attendance, and strive to cling to what is preached. He will persuade you not to come when you are most likely to get a blessing. Whenever you feel as if "Really, I cannot go again; for I am so often condemned, and find no comfort," say to yourself, "Now, I will go this time with all the more hope. Satan is laboring to prevent my going, because he fears that Christ will meet with me."

O, seeking mourner, do not forsake the courts of Zion, although you flood them with your tears. Be found where the gospel note tells of Jesus. Be found at the prayer meetings. Be found on your knees. Be found with your Bible open before you, searching for the promise, and above all, believe that Jesus came to save such as you are, and cast yourself upon Him.

Many ransomed ones have been enabled to enter the temple a little way. At the entrance of the holy place stood *the laver* full of water, where the priests habitually washed themselves. He who frequents the courts of Zion will often mourn at that laver, for he will say, "O, that I should need such washing! Cleanse me, O God. Wash me day by day. Dear Savior, cleanse me from secret faults." These mourners are deeply grieved at what others consider little spots, for sin hurts their tender consciences, and in the light of God sin is seen to be exceeding sinful in those whom God so highly favors.

Close to the laver stood *the altar*, where they offered the animal sacrifices. Now, he who sees the one great Sacrifice by which sin was put away, while he rejoices in the finished atonement, also laments the sin that slew the Substitute. Many a time may you hear the plaintive song—

> Alas! And did my Savior bleed?
>   And did my Sov'reign die?
> Would He devote that sacred head
>   For such a worm as I?[8]

The surer we are of our pardon the more we mourn over our sin. We look on Him whom we have pierced, and a mourning takes hold upon us like the mourning of Hadadrimmon in the valley of Megiddo when Judah lamented the best of kings and saw her sun go down in blood.[9] Awakened souls mourn for Jesus as one that is in bitterness for his first-born.

You can never stand at the altar and see Jesus bleed without your own heart bleeding, if, indeed, the life of God is in you. Can any but a heart of stone be unmoved at the sight of Calvary? Blessed are they who, in the middle of their joy for pardoned guilt, wash the pierced feet of Jesus with tears of love and grief.

Further on in the holy place, as you will remember, there stood *the altar of incense*. It was placed before the veil, which hid the holy of holies; but that veil is rent. Now, they who mourn in Zion often stand and weep as they think of Him whose prayers are the incense which God accepts—even Jesus, by whose intercession we live.

They think, "Oh! That I should be so cold in prayer when Jesus pleads so earnestly." They look over their own intercessions, and they see such faultiness, such wandering of thought, such coldness of heart, such forgetfulness, such pride, such want of faith, such utter unworthiness, that they cannot help deeply mourning. Besides, they remember when

Satan desired to have them, and sift them as wheat, and would have destroyed them if Jesus had not prayed for them, and they mourn the state of heart that placed them in such jeopardy.

As by faith they perceive how sweet the merits of Jesus are, they remember their own ill savor and begin anew to loathe themselves. Their very sense of acceptance in the Beloved fills them with humiliation; it seems too wonderful that Jesus should do so much for them, and make them so sweet to the Lord.

Great love is a melting flame. When we nestle like doves in the bosom of our Lord we mourn like the loving turtle; we mourn because of the great love that makes us almost too happy. We rejoice with trembling, and feel both fear and exceeding great joy.

And then, those who entered the holy place would see a table covered with loaves of bread: it was called *the table of the shewbread*.[10] Our blessed Lord Jesus Christ is that bread, and we feed on Him, as the priests of old did on the shewbread; but I confess I never stand there myself and think of how He feeds my soul with Himself without mourning that I have not a larger appetite for Him, and that I do not more continually feed upon Him.

I lament that ever I hoped to find bread elsewhere, or tried to feed on the swine-husks of the world. O, to hunger and thirst after Christ, for this is to be blessed! O, to feed upon a whole Christ, even to the full, for this is to be satisfied with royal dainties.

We cannot feed on Jesus without mourning that others are starving, and that we are not more eager to bring them to the banquet; that we are not ourselves more familiar with heaven's Bread, so as to know how to hand it out, that the dying multitudes of our great cities may be fed. O, Lord, cause your people more and more take to heart the sad fact that millions are famishing for want of the Bread of heaven.

Within the holy place also stood *the seven-branched candlestick*, which was always burning and giving forth its pearly light; before it we also mourn. When we rejoice in the light of God's Holy Spirit we cannot help mourning over our natural darkness, and our former hatred of light. We mourn to think, also, that we ourselves shine with so feeble a ray that our light does not so shine before men as to glorify God to the fullest extent.

We cannot enjoy the light of the divine Spirit without praying that we may have more of it. We acknowledge that if we have but little of it, it is our own fault, for He is ready to light us up with a splendor that shall make the sons of men to wonder from where such a luster came. We mourn, also, because the nations sit in darkness and the shade of death, and refuse the heavenly light.

And thus, you see, we mourn in Zion, from the entrance even to the innermost court.

Even when we pass through the rent veil, and stand at *the mercy seat,* and enjoy the believer's true place and privilege, we still mourn. We think of the law, covered by the propitiatory,[11] and we mourn our breaches of it. We think of the pot of manna, and mourn the days when we called the heavenly food "light bread."

We remember Aaron's rod that budded, and say to ourselves, "Sadly, it is a memorial of my own rebellion as well as of my Lord's power." We ask ourselves, "Where is my pot of manna of remembered mercy? Sadly, my rod does not bud and blossom as it should, but often it is dry and fruitless. That law which my Lord hid in His heart, how little respect have I had for it, or remembrance of it."

Then, looking at the golden mercy seat, we wet it with our tears because here the blood-drops fell, by which we are brought near. The glory of Jehovah between the cherubim bows us down, and we cry, "Woe is me, for I have seen the King, the Lord of hosts." Our impurity prostrates us when like Isaiah we behold the glory of the Lord. Is it not fitting that it should be so?

Thus, you see, from the outer courts of Zion right into the Holy of Holies, every spot suggests mourning, and true children of God yield to the influence of it. In every place of mercy or privilege that they occupy they look down upon themselves with shame and confusion of face.

Mr. Dyer used to say, "When the peacock shows his fine feathers he ought to recollect that he has black feet and a horrible voice." Truly, whenever we are full of divine graces and blessings, it is good to recollect what we are by nature and what impurity still lurks within us, so that we may be humble and, with our confidence in Jesus, may mingle repentance of sin.

III. And now, thirdly, WHO THINKS OF THESE MOURNERS? Who equips those who mourn in Zion? Who looks upon poor and needy souls? Very often their friends avoid them: if they mourn much and long, their friends shun their society, and their familiar acquaintances know them no more.

There are places of worship where mourners in Zion might come and go by the year together, and no one would utter a sympathetic word; a broken heart might bleed to death before any hand would offer to bind it up. I love to see Christian people concerned about poor mourners and eager to meet with penitent and desponding ones. It ought not to be possible, dear friends, in an assembly of believers, for a mourning soul to come and go many times without some Barnabas—some son of consolation—seeking him out and offering a word of good cheer in the name of the Lord. But mark this—whoever forgets the mourner, the Lord does not.

There are three divine persons who remember the mourner. The first is *the eternal Father.* Read the first part of Isaiah 61:1: "The Spirit of the Lord GOD is upon me; because *the LORD* hath anointed me to preach good tidings unto the meek; he has sent me to bind up the broken-hearted." God, the ever-blessed Father, pities His sorrowing children and has respect unto their prayers.

Poor soul, you are deeply wounded because of your sin, and no one on earth knows it; yet your heavenly Father knows the thoughts of your heart, and He tenderly sympathizes with your anguish of mind. Where are you standing, poor fretting Hannah, you of a sorrowful spirit? I come not, like Eli, to judge you harshly and censure you unjustly.

Where are you? Do you mourn and sigh after your Lord? Then go in peace. The Lord grant you your petition. It shall surely be done unto you according to your faith. God, the eternal Father, first of all, remembers those who mourn. "...I *am* poor and needy; *yet* the Lord thinketh upon me...."[12]

Moreover, *God the Son* has the same kind thoughts towards His mourners. What does the first verse say? "The Spirit of the Lord GOD is upon me"; and you know that it is Christ who speaks. "The Lord hath anointed me to bind up the broken-hearted." Jesus, then, undertakes the cause of the troubled. He was a mourner all His days, and therefore He is very tender towards mourners.

> He knows what fierce temptations mean,
> For He felt the same.

"I know their sorrows," He is saying. "In all their affliction he was afflicted."[13] He was made perfect through sufferings. Rejoice, O mourner, for the Man of Sorrows thinks upon you.

And then *the Holy Spirit*—the third person of the blessed Trinity—according to the text—remembers mourners. "The Spirit of the Lord GOD is upon me," He says, "because the LORD hath anointed me." Yes, blessed Spirit, You are the Comforter, and whom can You comfort but mourners?

It would be useless to comfort those who never knew a sorrow, superfluous to attempt to offer consolation to those who never were depressed. The Holy Spirit hovers like a dove over the assemblies of the Sabbath, and wherever He finds a heart that is broken with a sense of sin, He alights there and brings light and peace and hope.

Be of good courage, then, you mourners, for the three divine Persons unite on your behalf: the One God thinks upon you, and the gentleness and tenderness of His almighty heart are moved towards you. Is not this good cheer?

IV. Our fourth and last point is this, WHAT DOES THE LORD DO FOR THEM?—"*To appoint unto them that mourn in Zion.*"

Let us take first the ordinary rendering of the text—"*To appoint* unto them." God makes appointments to bless mourners. It is His decree, His ordinance, and His purpose to bless those who mourn in Zion.

Some mourners are greatly frightened at predestination; they are afraid of the divine decrees. Be of good comfort, there is no decree in God's great book against a mourner. "I have not spoken in secret, in a dark place of the earth: I said not unto the seed of Jacob, Seek ye me in vain."[14]

God's terrible decrees are against the proud, whom His soul hates, and He will break them in pieces; but as for the humble and the meek, His purposes concerning them are full of grace. Read the following verses of Isaiah 61 and see—"to give unto them beauty for ashes, the oil of joy for mourning, the garment of praise for the spirit of heaviness." It is registered in the record office above, and stands in His eternal book, and so must it be: "Blessed *are* they that mourn; for they shall be comforted."[15] When you think of the decrees remember this decree, and be of good comfort.

But an equally accurate rendering of the text is, "*To provide* for those that mourn in Zion." "To provide." God not only intends to bless, but He does bless His mourners. Our heavenly Father prepares good gifts for His mourning family.

For whom did Jesus die but for mourners? For whom does He live but for mourners? For whom are the blessings of His coming but for mourners? You who are troubled because of sin, and hate it, all God's heart goes out towards you, and all the riches of the everlasting covenant are yours. Boldly take them, since for mourners they are provided. For whom are clothes but for the naked? For whom are alms provided, but for the needy? For whom the bath, but for the filthy? For whom the medicine, but for the sick? For whom

God's grace, but for you that need it and mourn because of your need?

Come and welcome. May the Lord bring you to Himself at this very hour.

Last of all, the text may run thus, "*To arrange* for those that mourn." The Lord has arranged, settled, and appointed to bless those who mourn; His plans are laid for it, and the method and means are appointed. God has made all things ready to bless you that mourn.

The only actual preparation that is needed for Christ is that you should need Him; and the only conscious preparation is that you should feel your need, or, in other words, should mourn. Christ is full: are you empty? Then there is room for you. Christ is generous: are you poor? Then you are the person on whom He will bestow His gifts.

I think I see before me a beautiful tree loaded with fruit. Do you see it? There are the ruddy apples in profusion waiting to be gathered. The boughs are hanging down; the excess of fruit burdens them. The tree has a voice. I hear its leaves rustling with a request. If you could hear it speak, what would it say? "Baskets! Baskets! Baskets!" It is asking for baskets.

Well, here are a number of baskets. Some of them are full. Shall we bring them? No, they are of no use to the tree. But here is a poor basket which, if it could speak, would say, "I am utterly empty: I cannot be of any use to that beautiful tree which has such abundance of fruit upon it, while I have none." But, indeed, its use lies in its emptiness. Now, my brother, the Lord Jesus is that loaded tree, and He asks you simply to be an empty basket into which He may put the rich fruits of His life and death.

If you have a fullness of your own you may go your way; but if you have nothing whereof to glory, and if you desire to receive of His fullness, then you and the Lord Jesus are well met. Jesus Christ my Lord is willing to bestow His grace upon the most guilty of mankind; Jesus is able to lift up to the gates of heaven even those that lie up against the gates of hell.

Only trust Him. Only trust Him, you that mourn. Only trust Him, and you shall be comforted; for He has appointed, provided, and arranged all good things for you. May His Spirit lead you at once to partake of the table that He has furnished for mourners in Zion. Amen.

CHAPTER 4

Beauty for Ashes

To give unto them beauty for ashes...—*Isaiah 61:3b*

Again I would remind you that the mission of our Lord Jesus Christ related to mourners in Zion. He did not come into the world to exalt those who are high, to give greater power to the strong, or to clothe those who are already clad in their own righteousness. No, the Spirit of God was upon Him to preach good tidings to the meek, to bind up broken hearts, to redeem captives, and to release prisoners.

He came with blessings for the poor, not with luxuries for the rich. This ought to be a very great subject of thanksgiving to those who are heavy of heart. Is it not sweet to think that the Anointed of the Lord came for your sakes; that you of rueful countenance, whose eyelids are fringed with beaded tears, whose songs are dirges, who dwell at death's door, may be brought forth into the sunlight?

Most men choose cheerful company whereby they may be entertained, but the Lord Jesus evidently selects mourners, and delights in those whom He may encourage and cheer. Blessed be His name! How meek and lowly He is in all His ways! How forgetful of self and how thoughtful towards His poor servants. He looks upon them with a pitying eye, and makes untold blessings their portion.

Notice with pleasure that in dealing with mourners, according to the text before us, the Lord acts upon terms of exchange or barter. He gives them beauty for ashes, the oil of joy for mourning, and the garment of praise for the spirit of heaviness.

It is a gracious exchange, but it is tantamount to everything being a free gift. "To give unto them beauty for ashes" is a free gift, because what He takes away is of no value, and they are glad to be rid of it. In condescending compassion, He took our ashes upon Himself. Oh, how they once covered His sacred head and marred His beauty! He took our mourning, and it made Him the Man of Sorrows in the day of His humiliation! He took our spirit of heaviness; as He lay prostrate in the garden beneath the load, He was exceedingly heavy and sorrowful even unto death. He took a loss to give us a gain.

So, it is a barter in which there is a double profit to us. We lose what was loss, and the gain is pure gain. From our Lord the blessings of love are all of free grace, and therefore let Him have all the praise.

I am sure that no mourner would hesitate to deal with Jesus on these special terms that only divine love could have thought of. If you have ashes, will you not be glad to exchange them for beauty? If you are mourning, will you not willingly cease from weeping to be anointed with the oil of joy? And if the spirit of heaviness presses upon you like a nightmare, will you not be glad to be set free and to be arrayed in the glittering garments of praise?

Yes, there could not be better terms than those that grace has invented. We accept them with delight. Poor mourner, they are specially ordained for you, so that: by the removal of evil from you and the bestowing of good upon you, a twofold grace might doubly enrich and comfort you.

In our present meditation, I call attention, first, to *the lamentable condition* in which many of the Lord's mourners are found: they sit in ashes, expressive of deep sorrow. Second, we shall observe *the divine interposition* on their behalf, for the ashes are removed. Third, we shall notice *the sacred gift*—"beauty for ashes."

I. Let us begin with THE MOURNER'S CONDITION—he is covered with ashes as the emblem of his sad condition. Let us now, like Cinderella, sit down amongst the cinders awhile, so that we may come forth from the ashes with something better than glass slippers, adorned with a beauty that shall befit the King's courts. The fairytale that has often made our childhood smile shall now be actually realized in our own souls. Yes, we shall see how far truth outshines romance and how much grander are the facts of God than the fictions of men.

It seems, from the text, that *the righteous are sometimes covered with grief.* Peoples of the Orient were always excessive in the use of symbols, and therefore, if they were in sorrow, they endeavored to make their outward appearance describe their inward misery. They took off all their soft garments and put on sackcloth, and this they tore into rags. Then, upon their heads, instead of perfumed oil, which they were so fond of using, they threw ashes, thereby disfiguring themselves and making themselves objects of pity.

Ashes were old emblems of mourning, and they continued to be so down to Popish time, of which we have a trace in the day called Ash Wednesday, which was the commencement of the time of fasting known as Lent. It was supposed that those who began to fast sat in ashes to begin with. Such symbols we leave to those who believe in the bodily exercises and outward rites of worship.

However, God's servants have their spiritual fasts, and their heads are metaphorically covered with ashes. I will not stop to read you the list of the occasions in which the princes of the royal blood of heaven are found sitting in the place of humiliation and distress. Suffice it to say that *they began their new life among the ashes.* Like Jabez, who was more honorable than his brothers, they were born in sorrow.

Some of us will never forget our grief for sin: it was a bitterness with which no stranger could interfere. We shall never forget the anguish of our soul and our deep humiliation, which no ashes could sufficiently symbolize. Like the patriarch of old, we cried, "I abhor *myself*, and repent in dust and ashes."[1]

Repentance since then has always had a large degree of mourning connected with it: sorrow has salted all our penitential tears. It is right it should be so; and it is equally right that we should never stop repenting. Repentance and faith are two inseparable companions. They flourish or decay together like the two arms of the human body.

If faith could enter heaven, repentance would certainly pass through the gate at the same time. Whether or not they will both enter there, or something like them, I will not venture to declare quite so confidently as some have done. I will not positively say that in eternity I shall regret that I have sinned and shall still believe in Jesus and find my everlasting safety in so doing. But, if I did so declare, who could disprove it?

Surely we shall mourn for sin as long as we are upon the earth, and we do not desire to do otherwise. Grief for sin and love to Jesus will endure through life. There will never come a time when we shall refuse to bathe with tears the pierced feet and kiss them with warmest love.

> Sorrow and love go side by side;
> Nor height nor depth can e'er divide
>   Their heaven-appointed bands.
> Those dear associates still are one,
> Nor till the race of life is run
>   Disjoin their wedded hands.[2]

We have to mourn bitterly when we have fallen upon times of strong temptation and of surprising sin. We grieve to confess the fact, but it is sadly true that faults have overtaken us. Who among God's chosen sheep has not gone astray? Consequently, we have had to return to the sackcloth and the ashes, and our heart has sunk within us.

By reason of our old nature we have transgressed like David, and then by reason of our new nature we have wept like David, and mourned our broken bones. If a soiled spot has defiled our garments, we have been led by the Holy Spirit to go at once to Jesus. And while He has washed it out with His blood, we have lamented our offence. Whenever believers permit the fires of sin to burn, before long they are made to cast the ashes of repentance upon their heads and shrink into the dust.

Beloved friends, we have also covered our heads with ashes because of the sins of others. Parents have been compelled to sorrow very grievously for their sons and daughters. The wail of David is no unusual sound. "O Absalom, my son, my son! Would God I had died for thee, O Absalom, my son, my son!"[3]

Many a woman sits in ashes half her life because of her ungodly husband, who makes her life bitter to her. Many a loving sister pines inwardly because of a profligate brother who persists in ruining himself. The crimes of the world are the burdens of the saints. We cannot make the ungodly mourn for their guilt, but we can and do deeply mourn over their lack of deep feeling.

How can we bear to see our fellowmen choosing everlasting destruction, rejecting their own mercies, and plunging themselves into eternal misery? If Hagar said, "Let me not see the death of the child,"[4] and if the prophet's eye ran with ceaseless tears over the slain of his people: shall we not mourn in dust and ashes the willful soul-suicide of our neighbors who, with mercy at their doors, perish before our eyes?

Moreover, we pity the Christian who does not frequently mourn over the depravity of the times in which he lives. Infidelity has in these last days stolen the garb of religion, so that now we frequently come upon books in which the fundamentals of the faith are denied, written by ministers of churches whose professed creed is orthodox.

Our grandfathers would have shuddered at reading from a disciple of Tom Paine sentiments that pretending ministers of the gospel have given forth to the world. Things have reached a painful place when those who are called to proclaim the gospel are allowed to use their position to sow doubt about it and to sap and undermine all belief in it. Such conduct is meanness itself. It is beyond understanding that the churches tolerate it.

Only Satan himself could have put it into a man's heart to become a salaried preacher of the gospel in order to deny its fundamental truths. He who does this is *Judas Redivivus*, Iscariot the Second. God save us from all complicity with such practical falsehood and fraud!

When the child of God sees these things, and also sees ritualism and tolerance of error spreading on all sides, he feels sympathy with Mordecai. Of him we read: "When he perceived all that was done, he rent his clothes and put on sackcloth with ashes, and went out into the midst of the city, and cried with a loud and bitter cry."[5]

It would be a happy sign if there were more of this, and especially if many were found to imitate Daniel, who said, "I set my face unto the Lord God, to seek by prayer and supplications, with fasting, and sackcloth, and ashes."[6] We should soon behold the dawn of better days if such ashes were commonly found upon saintly heads.

Yes, the best of God's people must sometimes sit down among the ashes and cry, "Woe is me." When the saints mourn, it will sometimes happen that they cannot help showing their sorrow; it is too great to be controlled or concealed. Usually a spiritual man tries to conceal his soul's distress, and he has his Master's command for doing so, for Jesus said: "But you, when you fast, anoint your head and wash your face, so that you do not appear to men to be fasting."[7]

In personal trouble we would rather bear our burden alone than load others with it, and therefore we endeavor to maintain a cheerful manner even when our heart is sinking like a millstone in the flood. As to spiritual depressions, we cannot show these to men who know nothing about them; and in the presence of the ungodly we are speechless upon such topics. Yet there are sorrows that will have a voice, concerning which we may even be told to speak. As the prophet says, "O daughter of my people, gird *thee* with sackcloth, and wallow thyself in ashes."[8]

At such times we must express our inward grief, and then the men of the world begin to ask, "What's wrong with him?" and to cry jeeringly, "He is melancholy; religion has turned his brain." Only the other night, a mother said, "What makes Jane so sorrowful?" She did not know that her daughter was under a sense of sin.

Your colleagues, my good friend, asked you the other morning, "What makes you so dull?" They did not comprehend that their vile language had helped to aggravate and wound your heart, so that it was bleeding inwardly.

As we have joys that those of the world cannot share, so we have sorrows that they cannot comprehend. Yet we are obliged now and then to let them see that we are sad, even though this brings us new reproach. The ashes must sometimes be upon our head, and we must cry, "They have heard that I sigh...all mine enemies have heard of my trouble."[9]

Therefore, dear friends, when you see a mournful believer, do not condemn him or fail to appreciate him; for his sorrow may be a necessity of nature. Yes, it may even be a direct result of his eminence in grace. He may, perhaps, love the souls of men more than you think. He may have a more tender sense of the sinfulness of sin than you have. And perhaps if you knew his family trials, and if you knew the jealousy others have regarding his walk with God, or if you knew how the Lord has hidden His face from him, you would not wonder at his rueful countenance.

You might even marvel that he is not more cast down, and you might be ready to give him your pity and even your admiration, instead of your cold censure. Be sure of this, that some of the holiest of men have mourned as David did: "I have eaten ashes like bread, and mingled my drink with weeping."[10]

Next let us note that *such grief disfigures them*. I draw that conclusion from the contrast intended by the words of our text—"beauty for ashes." Ashes are not beautifiers, and mournful faces are seldom attractive.

A believer in a mourning frame of mind wears a marred countenance. He is disfigured before his friends; he makes bad company for them, and they are likely to see his weak points. He is disfigured before his fellow Christians: whereas they delight to see a brother rejoicing in the Lord—a manifest token of favor—sorrow of heart is often contagious, and therefore it is not admired.

The mourning Christian is especially disfigured in his own esteem. When he looks in the mirror and sees his repentant reflection, he cries to himself, "'Why art thou cast down, O my soul?'[11] If I am alright within, why do I feel this way?"

He questions, upbraids, and condemns himself. If his eyes were not so weakened by tears he might see a beauty in his sorrow. Yet, at the moment he cannot. Rather, he views himself as a mass of unattractiveness. And, he is not altogether wrong, for generally with spiritual mourning there is a measure of real disfigurement.

Unbelief, for instance, is a terrible blot upon anyone's beauty. Distrust of God is a horrible blotch. Discontent exceedingly injures mental and spiritual loveliness. We are not lovely when we are unbelieving, petulant, envious, or discontented. We are not beautiful when we are distrustful and suspicious, self-willed, and rebellious. Yet these evils often go with soul sorrow. We may truthfully say that some Christians are not only at times very sorrowful, but also their beauty is marred by their misery.

The grief of good men's hearts *is often a very expressive one*, as the language before us suggests. When sorrow puts ashes on its head, what does it say? It makes the man eloquently declare that he feels that he is as worthless as the dust and ashes of his house.

"I cover my head," he says, "with ashes to show that the very noblest part of me—my head, my intellect—is a poor, fallen, earthly thing of which I dare not boast: I count the best thing there is in me to be but dust and ashes suitable only to be cast away."

You mourners often thus despise yourselves. Therefore, if it is any consolation to you to know it, I know a minister of Christ who the longer he lives thinks less and less of himself, and utterly abhors himself before God. It is a wonder of divine grace that the Lord should ever have loved us at all, for there is nothing in our nature that is lovely.

Through our fall there is everything in us to be hated by His pure and holy mind, but nothing to esteem. And the best of the best, when they are at their best, are poor creatures. Lord, "What is man, that thou art mindful of him?"[12] If the righteous Judge had swept the whole race away at the beginning with the great, flooding destruction, He would still have been as great and glorious and blessed as He is; He only spares us because He is infinite in mercy.

When Abraham said, "I have taken upon me to speak unto the LORD, I that am but dust and ashes,"[13] he did not have too lowly an opinion of himself; for even the father of the faithful, though a prince among men, was nothing in himself but a son of fallen Adam. Nothing but undeserved mercy made him different from the idolatrous race out of which he was chosen and called. "Earth to earth, ashes to ashes" is our last memorial, and, all along, we are tending that way by nature, for we are of the earth, earthy. When we put ashes on our head we confess ourselves to be what we really are.

The use of ashes would seem to indicate that the fire is out. Men would not place burning coals upon their heads, but when they cast ashes there, they mean to say, "These ashes from which all fire is gone are like us: we too are spent, our fire of hope has burned out, our joy, our confidence, our strength have all departed from us, and left us only the black ashes of despair."

Is not this suggestive of a state of feeling common to truly humbled men? Let me ask, my brethren, have you not felt as if your coal were quenched in Israel? Have you not admitted that you had no hope whatever, apart from any salvation that might come to you from your dear Lord and Savior? Have you not felt as if every spark of faith and love and gratitude, and all that was good, was gone out in darkness?

Some of you young Christians have never yet stumbled into that bog, and I hope you never will. If you ever do, it may console you if I let you know that older saints have been there before you, and have had to cry to the strong for strength or they would have perished. Some of us know what it is to feel as if we had not even a spark of grace left. We cry,

"If aught is felt,
'Tis only pain to find we cannot feel."

At such times, we have felt that if there was any prayer in us it was only a prayer to be helped to pray, or to be helped to mourn that we could not pray—for our stock was lying dead, and our poor husbandry yielded us no increase, for want of dew from above. Our soul has been in a state of drought, the rain from heaven has been withheld, and the earth has broken and cracked beneath our foot, devouring rather than nourishing the seed. God's children have their droughts and famines. At such times, dust and ashes are fitting emblems of their dry and dead condition.

Ashes, too, as the symbol of sorrow, might also indicate having passed through the fire of trial, even as these ashes have been burned. Truly, some of God's best servants have been most often through the furnace, and have been so long in the heat that strength fails them, and hope nearly expires. They cry to God for patience to endure all His holy will, yet they feel that their own power is as much spent as if they were burnt to nothing but ash, and there was nothing more left of them upon which the fire could kindle.

Is it not a mercy that the Lord looks upon such as these—the utterly spent ones who are ready to be blown away and to perish, even as smoke and dry ashes are borne away by the wind and lost?

You who are at ease in Zion know little about these terrible feelings. You should be grateful to God and sympathize with those who are more exposed to tribulation than you are. Join with them in magnifying the Lord because He promises beauty instead of these ashes of the furnace.

Ashes, also, as you know, are the emblem of death. The Romans placed the ashes of the dead in sepulchral urns. We say, "Dust to dust, ashes to ashes," when we bury the departed. It is not uncommon for tested saints to complain that they are brought into the dust of death by a faintness of mind that renders life a difficulty. We come to look upon the grave as a refuge and a relief. "Oh," cries one, "they may as well bury me, for I am more dead than alive. I may as well heap ashes on my head." Like Elijah they say, "Let me die, for I am no better than my fathers!"[14]

To such depths of grief the best of men have sometimes descended. Many of the most peaceful and joyous spirits have joined in David's description of himself—"I am as a man *that hath* no strength, Free among the dead, like the slain that lie in the grave, whom thou rememberest no more: and they are cut off from thy hand."[15]

Enough of this sad tone; let us change the subject. We have shown you the believer in the ashes; let us now rejoice that some better thing is in store for him.

II. Secondly, there is A DIVINE INTERPOSITION. The Lord breaks in upon the mourner's misery, and makes the most gracious arrangements for his consolation. When a man is in sore trouble, he naturally begins to look this way and that way for deliverance; thereby, much of the man's mind and heart are made manifest. You may readily judge whether you are a child of God or a hypocrite by seeing in what direction your soul turns in seasons of severe trial.

The hypocrite flies to the world and finds a sort of comfort there, but the child of God runs to his Father, and expects consolation only from the Lord's hand. True grace abides with God and submits itself to His will. This is always good for us.

Brother, if the Lord causes you to be sick, remain sick until the Lord restores you, for it is dangerous to call in any other physician to your soul but your Lord. If the Lord frowns, do not ask others to smile, for you can derive no joy from that source. If God's wrath breaks you, let God's love mend you, or else remain broken. "I will not be comforted till Jesus comfort me" is a sweet resolve of a truly penitent soul, for has not the Lord said, "I kill, and I make alive; I wound, and I heal; I the Lord do all these things."[16] Will you take the healing and the making-alive out of Jehovah's hand? God forbid! Where you have received your hurt, there get your comfort. Where you drink the gall of sorrow, there drink the wine of joy; for in the Lord's hand there is abundant mercy to be found, and He will end your misery.

According to the text, the way in which believers rise out of their mourning is through *the coming of Jesus*. Read Isaiah 61 again. What does the Lord say? "The Spirit of the Lord GOD is upon me; because the LORD hath anointed me." Yes, beloved, our hope lies in the mission of Christ, in the person of Christ, in the work of Christ, in the application of the blood of Christ to our hearts. We turn our eyes evermore towards the hills: from there, comes our help.

Look always, O sinner, to the brazen serpent, no matter what serpent bites you. Whether it is the old serpent himself, or some smaller serpent of the same brood that lurks in the way and bites at the horse's heels, still look to the one appointed cure. Never speculate in healing drugs, but keep to the one antidote that never fails. Jesus is the consolation of Israel, and may Israel place her hope nowhere else.

And, notice that it is Jesus coming *in the gospel* that is the mourner's hope: for this coming of the Lord is to preach good tidings to the meek, and so to bind up the broken-hearted. I have little confidence in people who speak of having received *direct* revelations from the Lord, as though He appeared otherwise than by and through the gospel. His word is so full, so perfect, that for God to make any fresh revelation to you or me is quite needless. To do so would be to put a dishonor upon the perfection of the sure word of testimony. In "the most sure word of testimony," there is a release from every difficulty, an ointment for every sore, and a medicine for every disease.

My dear, sorrowing friend, it is very dangerous to look for consolation from dreams, from opening the Bible to certain texts, from imagined voices, or from any other foolish superstitions in which weak-minded persons seek comfort. Rather, go to what God has said in the Scriptures. When you find your character described there and promises made to one like you, then take those promises home to your heart, for they are plainly spoken to you.

Do not look for comfort in clouds of fantasy or moonlight superstition; believe in the Lord Jesus, who comes to bless broken hearts in no other way than by preaching to them the glad tidings of His grace. You are not to expect the Lord Jesus to speak with you in any other way than by the written Word applied to the soul by the Holy Spirit.

Look for no new revelation; drive out the very idea as deceptive. If an angel were to come to my chamber and inform me that he brought a message from God that would tell me more than is written in the Scriptures of truth, I would not listen to him for a moment; rather, I would say, "Get you behind me, Satan. The end of these manifestations has come: the stars no more appear, for the sun has risen."

Our heavenly Father has already sent the Lord Jesus, and it is written, "last of all He sent His Son."[17] In Christ Jesus, there is such a fullness of truth and grace that all the angels combined could not increase it. He who looks for more revelation should beware, for fear of receiving the curse with which the Bible concludes, which will certainly come upon any who either add to, or take from, the inspired words of God.

The sum of the matter is this—if there be any comfort to be received, it is in Christ, and if there be any ashes to be taken away, and any beauty to be given, it will be through the Lord Jesus in the preaching and reading of the Word. I say this as protest against the superstitions of weak minds.

But now I want you to notice something that does not appear in our English version of the text, but is clear in the Hebrew. It is that *the Lord very easily makes a change in His people's condition*, for the word in the Hebrew for ashes is *epheer*, and the word for beauty is *peer*.

The change is very slight in the original. Some idea of the similarity of the words may be given you in English if I quote from Master Trapp:[18] "The Lord promises to turn all their sighing into singing, all their musing into music, all their sadness into gladness, and all their tears into triumph."

Perhaps I may give you a meaning closer to the Hebrew by saying, He turns our mourning into morning. In the case before us we might say, "He gives us splendors for cinders"—beauty for ashes. As readily as we change a word by a single letter, so easily does the God of all comfort alter the condition of His people. With Him nothing is hard, much less impossible. From the cross to the crown, from the thorn to the throne, from misery to majesty is but a hand's turn with the Lord.

He often calls His people from sitting at the gate to riding upon the king's horse, like Mordecai; from lying in the dungeon to ruling in the land, like Joseph; from the dunghill to double wealth, like Job; from the caves of Engedi to the palace in Jerusalem, like David. This He does suddenly and easily, as when a man lights a candle and the darkness departs at once.

How charming and astonishing the change: to pass in a moment from winter into summer, from midnight into noon, from storm into profound calm! This is the finger of God, and it is often seen. Many have been able to join in the song of the psalmist:

> All through the night I wept full sore,
>   But morning brought relief;
> That hand, which broke my bones before,
>   Then broke my bonds of grief.
>
> My mourning He to dancing turns,
>   For sackcloth, joy He gives,
> A moment, Lord, Thine anger burns,
>   But long Thy favor lives.[19]

When you are at your lowest do not conclude that it will be months before you can rise. It is not so. From the nadir to the zenith you will spring at a single leap when the Almighty Helper girds you with power.

David in the psalms describes the Lord coming to his rescue in haste most marvelous. Out of the depths, he was snatched by the flash of Jehovah's power:

> On cherub and on cherubim
>   Right royally He rode,
> And on the wings of mighty winds
>   Came flying all abroad.
> And so deliver'd He my soul:
>   Who is a rock but He?
> He liveth—Blessed be my Rock!
>   My God exalted be![20]

How joyously David sings! And well he may after so special a rescue. There is no slow traveling with God when His people are in sorrow. Before they have time to call, He answers them; while they are yet speaking, He hears their requests. He hears them chanting, "*De Profundis*," and He lifts them to sing aloud, "*Gloria in Excelsis*"; from "Out of the depths" their tune changes to "Glory in the highest." There are no slow pauses of weary hope. The Lord works a world of wonders in the twinkling of an eye.

Thus, we see how our Lord gives beauty for ashes.

III. We now turn to the last point, which is WHAT HE BESTOWS INSTEAD OF THE ASHES—beauty. All disfigurement is removed. The ashes had made the person to be defiled, uncomely to others, and unpleasant to himself; but all this is removed. Beauty is given, and his countenance is not marred with dust and grime. His face is bright with joy and beaming with hope.

No more unpleasant to the eye, the person has even become attractive and delightful. The original Hebrew implies that occasions for joy and emblems of joy are also given, for it might be read, "A garland for ashes." The ashes were on the head, and now a crown is placed there. The allusion is to the nuptial tiara worn by men on their marriage day.

The Lord's mourners are to be decked with crowns of delight instead of being disfigured with ashes of grief. When does that happen to us? Do you remember when you first got a sense of forgiveness? How gloriously were you then arrayed! When the father said of his prodigal son, "Bring forth the best robe and put *it* on him, put a ring on his hand, and shoes on *his* feet,"[21] that was a high day; and so it was with us when we also were delivered from our filthy rags and clothed in righteousness divine. Our ashes were gone, then, and a crown adorned our heads. Forgiven! It was a joy of joys. Even now as we look back upon it we begin to sing again:

> Happy day! Happy day!
> When Jesus washed my sins away.[22]

We went a little farther on in spiritual life, and then we discovered that we were the children of God. We did not at first know our adoption: but it burst gloriously upon us like a newly kindled sun.

Do you remember when you first learned the meaning of the word, and perceived that adoption secured eternal salvation? For the heavenly Father does not cast His children away, nor can they cease to be the objects of His love. How can any child be *unchilded?* And, if still a child, he must be still beloved, and still an heir.

When you once drank consolation from that doctrine, did you not receive a tiara for ashes? How lovely a thing it is to be a child of God! "Behold what manner of love the Father hath bestowed upon us, that we should be called the sons of God!"[23]

We lived a little longer, and we began to understand the doctrine of vital union with Christ. We had not dreamed of it at the first. Then we discovered that there is a vital, actual, conjugal union between us and Christ—that we are married to Him. It is a great mystery, and it is a great truth. It is all but inconceivable that we should be members of His body, His flesh, and His bones; yet, it is so.

That was a heavenly day when we perceived that we were one with Jesus—"by eternal union one." Then we rejoiced as wearers of a marriage crown, and we sang:

My Beloved is mine and I am His.[24]

Since then we have learned other truths. On each occasion of being taught of the Lord, we have again obtained a crown for ashes. Another, and yet another, garland has adorned our brow. We have felt ourselves to be made priests and kings unto God, and the beauty of the Lord our God has rested upon us. All glory be to His name!

Beloved, reading the Word as our version does, our God has given us "beauty for ashes." Every child of God has the beauty of the imputed righteousness of Jesus Christ, and at this moment is all fair as he is viewed in Him who is altogether lovely.

Washed in Jesus' precious blood we are without a stain, and clothed in His righteousness we are accepted in the sight of God. O justified man, think of your ashes as a condemned sinner, and now think of the beauty that the righteousness of Christ has put upon you, and be astonished and carried away with delight.

Beside that, the Holy Spirit has given us a measure of sanctification or beauty of character. We know that we are not what we used to be. We are not what we want to be or what we shall be. Yet, there is a beauty about us now: in the fact of our being at heart wholly consecrated to God, in the repentance of sin, and the desire for holiness, which the Holy Spirit has created in us. Even the beginnings of holiness are beauty before God.

Then, brethren, we know there is a beauty put upon us by virtue of our union with Christ, for every member of Christ must be beautiful. See how even the spouse of the Old Testament, as she sang her song of love, though she could not have had a very clear sight of him in those dim days of types, which were only like a golden candlestick compared with the sun which shines on *us*, yet even she was enraptured with him.

She sings of him with unqualified admiration. From head to foot she delights in him, she perceives the very locks of his head, and the sandals of his feet to be beautiful, and she cries in rapture, "Yea, he *is* altogether lovely."[25] If, then you are a member of Christ, however lowly a part you are of Him, you are well pleasing and delightful in the sight of God.

Did you ever drink into your soul that amazing text, "Thou *art* all fair, my love; *there is* no spot in thee"?[26] It is the voice of the Bridegroom to the church He loves, and to the soul which is espoused to Him. As for myself, I appear to my own conscience to be spotted and defiled all over, and yet by faith I know that in Christ Jesus I am made to be spotless before the throne of God.

Concerning myself I cry, "Look not upon me, because I *am* black, because the sun hath looked upon me...."[27] I am become like a bottle in the smoke, my beauty has been eaten away like a garment eaten of the moth; and yet in Christ Jesus, together with the rest of His saints, I know that beauty is put upon me.

Though in ourselves deformed we are,
And black as Kedar's tents appear,

Yet when we put His beauties on,
Fair as the courts of Solomon.[28]

Blessed is he that understands this beauty that the Lord has given to us instead of ashes!

Let us remark that the contrast of our text is especially evocative, because it is not quite what we might expect. The Lord takes away our ashes, and what does He give in exchange? The natural contrast would be *joy*, but the Lord bestows that which is better, namely, *beauty*, because that is not only joy to us but also to others. "A thing of beauty," as we say, "is a joy forever." A beautiful person gives pleasure to all around.

Now, child of God, you are not only to have those ashes taken away which have previously disfigured you, but you are also actually to become the source of joy to others. How pleasant that will be for you who have been mourning so long that you have distressed your family.

Yes, young friend, you are to make your mother rejoice by telling her that you have found peace with God. You are yet to cheer your father's heart, young woman, when you shall say to him, "Father, I have found Him in whom you trust, and I am trusting in Him, too."

Yes, poor mourner, you will yourself be comforting other mourners one of these days. You who have been in Giant Despair's castle shall help pull down the monster's den. You can hardly believe it, but it shall be so.

In the sense of being a joy to others, many of the Lord's people are very beautiful indeed: you cannot help being charmed with them, especially with those of deep experience. Good men are glad of the company of those to whom the Lord has given the beauty of grace. Even the ungodly, though they do not confess it, have a respect for the majesty of holy characters.

There is a charm about beauty that makes her ride as on a lion through the midst of her foes; every man's hand is bound to defend her, and none dare to injure her. The beauty that the Lord gives to His people is as a queen among all beauties, and sways a potent scepter.

Yes, and when the Lord makes His people beautiful they are a delight even to God, for the Lord rejoices in His works. His grace-works are the noblest labor of His hands; and being fullest of grace, they are most graceful. The Lord delights in His people.

We read of the Lord Jesus, that His delights were with the sons of men, and even now, though angelic harps ring out His praises, He loves to be here in our churches, and to commune with us as a man speaks with his friend. Beloved, cultivate His society: abide with Him, and if He can find any cause of delight in you, which is a wonder of wonders, put all your delight in Him.

Let us have this gracious beauty about us, and even our heavenly Bridegroom will have to say,

> Turn away thine eyes from me,
>   for they have overcome me.
> Thou hast ravished my heart
>   with one look of thine eyes.[29]

May we be kept from marring this beauty, and be forever so fair that even our Lord Himself may look and love. Amen.

CHAPTER 5

The Oil of Joy for Mourning

The oil of joy for mourning....— *Isaiah 61:3c*

Mourners in Zion ought to be doubly comforted, for here is a second gift of love to them, a second exchange of loss for gain. The varied expressions of this choice Scripture show the manifold loving kindnesses of the Lord to His afflicted and the plentiful devices of wisdom by which He ministers consolation.

It was not enough to give the sorrowing ones BEAUTY FOR ASHES; He must add an oil with which to enhance the beauty, and take away, not only the ashes, but also the mourning that lay beneath them. This, also, illustrates the exceeding fullness of the blessings that are stored up in the Lord Jesus: in Him we have everything that the heart can wish, a rich variety of joyful blessings never to be exhausted.

This gift also shows us the marvelous fitness of our Lord Jesus, since solely because of His coming as the anointed of the Lord there is healing for the wounded, liberty for the captives, eyes for the blind, comfort for mourners, beauty for the disfigured, and oil for fading countenances. He meets every want of the soul, and fills the heart to overflowing with contented gratitude.

Let it be repeated and gratefully remembered: all these good things come by the anointed Savior alone. There can be no traffic with heaven except by the crimson road of the atoning blood and no channel for divine favor except by the

Christ of God, on whom the Spirit of the Lord forever rests. To Him be glory forever.

Blessed be His name, He is the channel of grace, and in Him is no narrowness or shallowness. Divine riches of glory flow to us by Christ Jesus.

> Immortal joys come streaming down,
> Joys, like His griefs, immense, unknown.

If our Redeemer were not what He is, what should we do? But being what He is, there is no necessity that He cannot supply, there is no grief that He cannot assuage, and there is no right desire that He cannot satisfy. Let us drink of the river of His fullness and sing to His praise.

Notice, also, at the outset of our present meditation, the effectual way in which the blessings that Jesus brings are bestowed upon mourners. We have often heard doubting ones say, "Yes, there are promises, but we cannot reach them. We know that there are abundant consolations, and comforts rich and free. But we do not feel their power, nor dare to take them to ourselves."

Now, in this place we see the condescending Lord Himself applying the oil of joy in exchange for mourning. His own right hand pours the precious oil upon the bowed head; He Himself causes the face to shine and banishes woe. A man may lie bleeding on the battlefield, and there may be ointments close at hand, but in his weakness and agony he may be unable to bind up his own wounds, or reach the medicines. He may die because he is not able to stretch so much as a finger to help himself to remedies that lie by his side.

It is an unspeakable mercy that our Lord gives His grace to us in such an effectual manner that His mourners actually obtain the help they need. He is a very present help, a real Comforter. The oil of joy is not shown to us in an unbroken alabaster vase, nor merely offered to us in a vial. It is actually and effectually applied to the soul.

Let us now come to the consideration of this second of the three great blessings bestowed upon the mourners in

Zion, and may we all enjoy a portion thereof while we meditate upon it.

I. In working out the metaphor, we shall observe that OUR LOVING LORD BRINGS HIS MOURNERS TO SIT AT A FEAST. This is clearly intended, for oil was largely used in the Orient upon festive occasions. The oil that makes man's face shine was associated with the bread, which strengthens man's heart, and the wine, which makes glad the heart of man, because these are the chief provisions of a banquet.

Before the feast or during the entertainment, the guests were refreshed with perfumed oil, which would be either poured upon the head or furnished for anointing the face. It was part and parcel of a great feast. Hence, we read of those who "drink wine in bowls, and anoint themselves with the chief ointments."[1] Therefore, our first thought is that the Lord Jesus brings mourning souls to a feast of love, at which they sing, "Thou preparest a table before me in the presence of mine enemies: thou anointest my head with oil."[2] How great will be our joy if we can feel that our Lord has brought us into His banqueting house, and that we are now reclining there.

Now to all believers this is truly the case. Our hunger now is assuaged, for He satisfies our mouth with good things. That fierce, wolf-like hunger, which we once felt, is gone forever; for it is written, "He that eats of this bread shall never hunger."[3] Our craving, all-consuming thirst is ended; for he that drinks of the water that Jesus gives him shall never thirst.

Many of Zion's mourners are sitting under the Word, longing for divine provision, and praying, "Lord, evermore give us this bread." The bread is theirs, and a voice cries to them, "Eat, O friends; drink, yea, drink abundantly, O beloved."[4] Your deadly famine of heart is gone, and the spiritual hunger which you now feel is a pleasant appetite, which gives a zest to heavenly food—an appetite that you long to have increased to the utmost.

Even at this moment, though you feel a blessed hunger and thirst after righteousness, you are filled with royal delicacies. You are no longer starving in the streets, nor famishing under the hedges and in the highways. By divine grace you have been sweetly compelled to come in, and you are at this moment the guests of the table of boundless mercy, where the name of Jesus is as ointment poured forth, so that all around you the oil of gladness is shedding a divine perfume.

You are no longer feeding the swine, but resting at the Father's table: the oxen and the fatlings are killed, and you are actually at the supper. Believe this, and act accordingly. And what a feast it is! For who is your host? The Lord of life and glory ordains "the feast of fat things, of fat things full of marrow, of wines on the lees well-refined."[5]

"The King sits at His table."[6] It is His table, and He sits at it. It is a great thing to dine with a king, but what must it be to be eating daily bread at the table of the King of kings? Let the joy-bells ring in your soul at the very thought, for you are already come to the great feast which the King has made for His Son. The King Himself comes in to see the guests. It is *the* feast of the universe. There never was such another, and there never can be. It is the foretaste of the great Supper of the Lamb. What provisions are put upon the table! Men do eat angels' food when they come here. Yes, they eat morsels better than the bread of angels, for the body of Christ has become the meat and the drink of His mourners.

Poor souls, you feast upon incarnate Deity. Speak of oxen and of fatlings? These are poor types compared with the wondrous provision of celestial grace with which the infinite Jehovah has loaded the table of the covenant. And all these things are yours. You may have as much as you will. There remains no need to eat bread by weight, nor to drink water by measure. He will satiate your soul with more than enough, and nothing shall be withheld from you. Ought you not to bless Him that you are now a guest at such a table, and that such food is at this very moment spread before you?

Think of your fellow guests. Look around you and inspect the company. Remember where you were a little while ago: you were strangers and foreigners. Yes, you were as dogs in the street. Where are you now? You are permitted to sit with the children of God, with the saints of the Most High. Does it not bring tears to your eyes to think that you— you who long refused to come, and despised the feast of grace—are, at last, brought in?

You sit at the feast of love, not only with God's people, but the saints above are also your companions now, for you have come "to the general assembly and church of the first-born, which are written in heaven, and to God the Judge of all, and to the spirits of just men made perfect...."[7] We eat with the glorious company of the apostles, the goodly fellowship of the prophets, the noble army of martyrs, and the holy church throughout the entire world. Now also we have fellowship with angels. We have come unto Mount Zion and to an innumerable company of angels.

Better still, we have fellowship with Jesus. "Jesus the Mediator of the new covenant"[8] is the center of the whole. It is His wedding feast, and we are glorifying Him by partaking of His Father's bounty. We cannot at this moment actually put our heads upon Jesus' bosom as John did, nor need we wish for that visible and physical delight. Yet, our heart rests upon His breast, and enjoys a bliss unspeakable in doing so. Jesus, Immanuel, we are safe in Your arms, and our heart is at perfect rest in You. We are even now abiding in You, while at Your Passover we keep the feast.

We are feasting with the great Father Himself. Beloved, when the glorious sacrifice becomes a meat offering, God Himself delights in it and partakes with us in the satisfaction made by His Son. Oh, the satisfaction that God the Father finds in Jesus! It is a theme upon which we dare not attempt to elaborate. But this we know: the Lord rests in His love; He smells a sweet savor in the person and work and sacrifice of

His dear Son. If we love Jesus, so does the Father; if we rest in Jesus, so does He; if we would gladly glorify Jesus, so would the Father.

Thus are we brought to feast with God, the Judge of all, when we come to "the blood of sprinkling, that speaketh better things than *that of* Abel."[9] Here the oil of joy is most befitting. Is it not most natural and proper that it should be poured out at such a festival?

II. We cannot linger, but must pass to this next observation: BEING AT A FEAST, WE SHOULD HAVE PRESENT JOY. Hence the text speaks of "the oil of joy for mourning." The mourning was present enough; the joy should be equally so. At feasts, the perfume poured upon the heads of the guests was a seemly and appropriate thing. It suited the feast; it made the guests feel at home; it gave refreshment all around as the delicious perfume sweetened the air.

Come, beloved, we have at this moment reason for joy, and let us use it. Let every child of God feel that he has the oil of joy, in the fact that he possesses present blessings. Our best things lie on the other side of the Jordan. We are looking for our full bliss at the coming of our Lord. Yet, we have much in the present. The oil of joy is on our faces now, our locks are even now damp with the sacred anointing, and it will be well for us to turn our thoughts towards that truth.

First, let all believers remember that we have today the joy of the atonement. "By whom also," says the apostle, "we have now received the atonement."[10] The atonement will be no more ours in heaven than it is now. "We have redemption by his blood."[11] Our sin will be no more put away in glory than it is at this moment, for our iniquity is even now cast into the depths of the sea. Our Substitute has finished transgression and made an end of sin. Having believed in Him, we know that for us the full atonement is already made and the utmost ransom forever paid. "It is finished." [12]

"Therefore, being justified by faith, we have peace with God."[13] "*There is* therefore now no condemnation to them which are in Christ Jesus...."[14] Having believed, we know that our sin is as far removed from us as the east is from the west. We know also that the righteousness of Christ is imputed to us and that it covers us from head to foot. This is a divinely sweet ingredient of the oil of joy, which now distills upon us from the head of our glorified Aaron, and perfumes even those who are as the skirts of his garments.

Besides that, my brother, at the present moment you live in the love of God. It may not be at this moment sensibly shed abroad in your heart by the Holy Spirit, but still "the Father himself loveth you."[15] If you are a believer in Christ, He will not love you more when you are in heaven than He loves you now, for He loves you infinitely at this instant. You are even now "accepted in the Beloved."[16]

"Beloved, now are we the sons of God."[17] Infinite love, eternal love, unchanging love, almighty love is the present possession of the children of God. Thus comes our safety; thus comes the certainty of the supply of all our wants; thus, indeed, flow all our joys. At this moment, despite our spirit depression and soul battling and heart strife, the Lord has set His love upon us and rests in that love. Should not this make our faces shine?

At this time, too, we possess the divine life within us. Having believed, we have been regenerated and the Spirit of God dwells in us. Yes, within these mortal bodies does the Godhead dwell. He has made our bodies to be the temples of the Holy Spirit. What a favor this is; for this indwelling is the witness of the Spirit within us, the perpetual seal of grace. God has put into us a new life, a life like His own; He has created in us a superior principle, unknown to flesh and blood, for we are not born again of the will of man, nor of the will of the flesh, but of the will of God. A supernatural life, which cannot die, has been implanted in us, because it is born of God. We have this and we know it, and because of it we greatly rejoice.

And not only so, but because we are the sons of God, we are heirs according to the promise, since it is written, "and if children, then heirs—heirs of God and joint-heirs with Christ."[18] Does not this oil make the face shine? What better delights can your imagination conceive than the divine joys of adoption? Oh, mourners, have you not here the oil of joy?

Further, we have the present joy of a high calling, involving the exercise of sacred functions. You are at this hour, beloved, as many of you as believe in Him, made kings and priests unto God. You are consecrated to the service of Him who has bought you with a price. The mark of the blood is upon you, and "ye are Christ's...."[19] At this moment, you are a living sacrifice bound with cords to the horns of the altar. Your Lord has sent you into the world, even as the Father sent Him into the world, to proclaim His truth and to do His will among the sons of men. Is not this cause for delight? Does not your divine vocation anoint you with the oil of gladness?

With this we have special privileges. There is one privilege I prize at this moment: I cannot tell you how much. It is this—the liberty to pray, the power to pray, the promise that I shall be heard. Take the mercy seat from me, and poverty, faintness, and anguish would seize my soul! As long as there is a mercy seat, a rent veil, and the voice that bids me draw near and tells me that if I wait upon the Lord I shall renew my strength, I have a joy worth worlds.

What, have you lost a child? Is your property melting before your eyes? Does health decline? Do friends forsake? Yet the throne of grace is accessible; fly to it, and lose your griefs. There, burdens are light, crosses bud with crowns, and tears sparkle into diamonds. Come here, you mourners, with the load of your doubts and fears. Supplication will quicken you, and in exchange for mourning, you shall obtain the oil of joy.

Time would fail me if I were to go through the whole catalogue of the sources of the Christian's present joy. Oh, worldling, you know, and we confess it is true, that our chief joys are yet to come. Notwithstanding, we have enough today to make us more than a match for you. You may display your present mirth and carnal delight if you will, and laugh at us who weep now. But we can endure your ridicule with calm complacency, because we have a secret peace and a deep fathomless repose of heart. They make us even now as far from envying you as an angel from envying a mole.

We are not of all men the most miserable, but of all men the most blessed. Our eternal hopes revive us amid the sorrows of this fleeting life. The harvests of heaven shake out and drop golden grain from above, upon which we feed even now. To have Jesus for our Brother, God for our Father, and the Spirit to be our Comforter is a better portion than the richest, the proudest, or the most famous worldly ones can possibly possess. The oil of joy is not made in the presses of earth: it drops upon us through the golden pipes of the sanctuary, flowing from the sacred olive trees that the Lord has planted.

III. Moving on, we offer a third observation, which is implied in the text: that THIS JOY COMES OF THE HOLY SPIRIT. This is clear, since always when we read of oil, we have before us, in Scripture, the divine influence of the Holy Spirit. "The Spirit of the Lord GOD is upon me, because the LORD hath anointed me." The oil with which Christ was anointed was the Holy Spirit. The oil of joy with which we are anointed is the same Spirit. It is He who gives us joy in the Lord.

The Holy Spirit brings joy to believers in this way. He first clears the understanding, and enables us to comprehend the deep things of God. Many poor souls know little about the precious blessings that the Lord has bestowed upon them. Up to now, although they are of the Lord's elect, they are not aware of it. Although they are among the redeemed of the Lord, they do not perceive it. There is light about them, and yet they cannot see, for their eyes are not yet opened beyond the power to see men as trees walking.

Let us be grateful if we have passed beyond this stage. Through infinite mercy the Holy Spirit has visited some of us. While He has painfully made us see our ruin, He has also most blessedly led us to comprehend something of the remedy, and has enabled us to understand with all saints what are the heights and depths, and to know the love of Christ, which passes knowledge. We have an anointing so that we know all things. Now are the mysteries opened, and the hidden things laid bare, and, therefore, we have joy in the Lord, for our renewed understanding floods our heart with rivers of delight.

The Holy Spirit also gives us joy by enabling us to exercise an appropriating faith. You that have faith, do you bless God sufficiently for it? Do we not fail to adore the divine mercy that has wrought this grace in us? We ought to blame ourselves when we find our faith to be weak. Yet, we must never commend ourselves when faith is strong. The weakness of faith is ours; the strength of faith comes of the Holy Spirit and of Him alone. Let us bless Him that He has enabled us to take to ourselves what the Lord Jesus has provided, so that now we do not only see His grace to be excellent, but we also grasp it as our own. Here is oil of joy for us indeed.

The Spirit also, very graciously, sanctifies us, and this is joy. It is a part of His work to discover sin in us and to excite a holy hatred of it. He burns in our soul like flames of fire consuming evil. Now, the destruction of sin is the destruction of sorrow; as a child of God grows in likeness to Jesus, he grows in solid peace of mind. If you will follow your doubts and fears to their roots, you will find that they grow from the dunghill of your sins. And when the Lord cleanses out the evil of our hearts, and creates a new spirit within us, the oil of joy perfumes the soul, and we are glad in His salvation.

Moreover, the Holy Spirit graciously quickens His people. What a wonderful effect quickening has upon our joy! Whenever we are slothful in the things of God, we miss the delights of healthy spiritual life, and before long we mourn. Yet, when the Holy Spirit comes and makes us feel lively, energetic, and sensitive, then we begin, also, to rejoice in the Lord. The power of His might within us works in us a leaping of holy joy. Those who not only have life, but also have it more abundantly, are highly favored, and know how to exult in the Lord.

Beloved, desire no joy but that which the Holy Spirit gives you. Thank God for the comforts of this life, but do not let them become your idols, as they will be if they become your exceeding joy. Draw from the upper fountains. Fill your pitcher at the eternal springs. Ask neither for the cinnamon nor camphor of this world's gardens. Rather, let your chief spices be the fruit of the Spirit, which are joy and peace through believing.

IV. We now notice that THIS JOY GIVES US A GREAT, PRESENT BENEFIT. I once heard someone say (very wickedly indeed, as I thought and still think) that sin could do the believer no harm. But he added, "Except that it destroys his comfort." I thought, "Well, that is a terrible 'exception' indeed; that surely is quite enough to fill us with holy fear. If anything robs the Christian of his joy, surely the loss is great enough to set him upon his watch tower."

Yet, I fear that many Christians do not consider this. They dream that it can be well with their souls when the joy of the Lord is gone. But, brethren, it is not so. The healthy condition of a child of God is a state of peaceful rest in the Lord. It is wonderful how full Scripture is of comfort for mourners, because the Lord's object is that the mourner may be comforted. "Comfort ye, comfort ye my people, sayeth your God. Speak ye comfortably to Jerusalem...."[20] Our Lord desired that we might have His joy fulfilled in us, and He said, "Let not your heart be troubled."[21] "Rejoice in the Lord always," said the apostle; as if that were not enough, he added, "*and* again I say, Rejoice."[22]

Hear me, you mourning ones—the maintenance of a cheerful, happy frame of mind is of the utmost importance to you, and for many reasons, which may be drawn from the

metaphor of oil. Oil is refreshing, and so is holy joy. It puts
new life into the soul, and renews its youth like the eagle's.
When the man is faint with long pursuing, he revives if he
perceives he already possesses present blessings in which he
may rejoice. The joy of the Lord is our strength.

Oil was intended also to make each guest agreeable to
his neighbors. When his head was anointed with the sweet
perfume, those round about him were gratified. Happy
Christians are pleasing to those about them. Thus, they
become a means of attracting souls to Jesus. We ought to be
so happy that others ask, "Where does their joy come from?"

If so, you can clearly see why we should exchange our
mourning for the oil of joy. It would be wrong to frighten
men from the glad tidings by drawing long faces and using
doleful tones.

Besides, brethren, you all know how weak you are in the
service of God if your heart runs down into despondency.
When holy joy comes back, you feel that you could face a
lion, or the old roaring lion himself. Joy makes us brave.
"The spirit of a man will sustain his infirmity; but a wounded
spirit who can bear?"[23] Give me the joyful Christian for his
Master's service, for he will break through a troop and leap
over a wall.

How gloriously does sacred joy lift you up above the
sorrows of the world! Yes, and even more, how it lifts you up
above earth's joys! The man who has once drunk the old
wine of the kingdom does not desire the new and sour wine
of earth. He who knows the joy of the Lord will despise the
joy of the world.

Earthly comforts are small concerns to the heavenly-minded.
They receive the comforts gratefully as ordinary gifts from
the Father's hand, while their hearts cry, "'The Lord *is* my
portion,' says my soul."[24]

He who has eaten the white bread of heaven has his
mouth put out of taste for the brown bread of earth. He who
has feasted at God's table, and had the oil of joy poured

upon his head by the Holy Spirit, has risen above the fascinations of the hour. What can charm a man who has gazed on the beauties of Jesus? What can delude us into idolatry when we have once beheld the glory of the Lord?

The joy of the Lord is a grand safeguard. Earnestly could I wish that all God's people were flooded with it. Then, there would be no fear of angry tempers, harsh speeches, or murmuring words. Full of the joy of the Lord, you would distain deeds of injustice in trade and grasping at the world. You would endure suffering with patience, and perform labor with diligence. Railing would never be returned for railing, or proud looks given to the poor. The joy of the Lord makes a man so calm, so quiet, and so heavenly that he lives above the world.

What a grand life is that of Abraham. He has his trials, and some of them are intense. Yet, he walks along the road of history with an almost noiseless tread, gliding along as though all were smooth. The record says, it came to pass that "the LORD had blessed Abraham in all things."[25] And yet, in the previous pages we read of trials with Lot, with Hagar and Ishmael, and the grand ordeal with Isaac. Faith made Abraham's trials blessings; and his inward joy, like Aaron's rod, swallowed up all the rods of his afflictions. The same road is open to us, and we have the same reasons for walking in it, since the God of Abraham is our God forever and ever. He who can live by faith shall have a constant supply of the oil of joy poured upon him by the Holy Spirit, and his mourning shall flee away.

V. Our last observation is THE JOY THAT GOD GIVES HIS PEOPLE IS BEST SEEN, AND FREQUENTLY BEST FELT, IN FELLOWSHIP. We began with noting that oil is connected with festivity; sweet spices are for banquets, where men feast together. Oh mourners, you will often find your souls made joyous when you assemble with your brethren. Bread eaten in secret is sweet, and morsels behind the door are delicious; yet, still the choicest and most abundant provisions are brought forth when the King's household gather around His table, and realize that "we *being* many are one bread."[26]

Personally, my happiest times are spent with my brothers and sisters in Christ in the high festivals, when the multitude keep holy day. Draw a circle around my pulpit, and you have hit upon the spot where I am nearest heaven. There the Lord has been more consciously near me than anywhere else. He has enraptured my heart while I have been trying to cheer and comfort His mourners. Many of you can say the same of your pew where you like to sit. It has been a Bethel to you, and the Lord Jesus has revealed Himself to you in the midst of His people.

Let us remember what delightful times we have had in prayer together. We have come into the sanctuary heavy of heart, and while one brother after another has approached the throne of grace for us, we have been unburdened and helped to joy in God till the prayer meeting has seemed to be a heaven below, a foretaste of the eternal meetings above. Thus the oil of joy is poured out in the assembly of fellowship. Many times, when we have been singing together some delightful hymn, in a lively, feeling manner, we have felt as if we could leap with delight, and so the oil of joy has streamed upon our heads. Have you not often cried with the poet:

> I would begin the music here,
>> And so my soul should rise;
> Oh for some heavenly notes to bear
>> My passions to the skies.

Yes, that is the oil of gladness given at the festival of praise among the sons of God. Who would not choose to be there?

A joyous influence has also been within the house when believers have met to talk with one another concerning the things of God in simple, devout conversation. Sadly, how little is there of such speaking one to another, especially among wealthy Christians. A Christian man remarked to me the other day that when he was a boy the good old Christian people were constantly talking about the doctrines of grace and other things concerning the kingdom of God, but there is little of this now.

The staunch old men of the last generation knew what they believed, and discerned between things that differed. They were, perhaps, a little too severe in their judgments; but still they did converse on divine things and were refreshed by doing so. But now we are so very charitable that we are afraid to talk to one another about the things of God, for fear we should differ. It should not be so, for when Christ is the subject, and God's people converse together, their hearts burn within them with sacred delight, and the oil of gladness is poured upon their heads. Holy fellowship brings heavenly joy. The conversation of saints with each other is the source of unnumbered delights.

Lastly, the communion table has been to many of us, above all other places in the world, the palace of delight. There are certain ones of us who never forget the ordinance for a single Lord's Day. And years of experience bear witness to the value of this means of grace. It is surprising that so few even among Christians are regular in their attendance at that thrice-blessed supper. A young girl said to me the other Sunday, "Jesus seems so near when we are at the table." She was quite right. The emblems used at the supper so vividly bring our Lord before us that we think only of His passion, of the blood that was shed, and of the body which was made to suffer for our sins.

Then are we borne away with grateful emotion and feel as if we had reached the very gate of heaven. While we drink the wine and eat the bread, our Lord Himself pours the oil of gladness upon us. You who neglect that ordinance are losing a great privilege, and, besides that, you are neglecting a solemn duty. May the Lord convince you of your negligence and bring you to delight in that ordinance, which is the joyful means of communion with Him.

Thus far, I have been talking to God's people, and you will say, "Have you not a word for the sinner?" Well, I have all along been speaking to the sinner, too; because all this is for you if you repent of sin and believe in the Lord Jesus Christ. If you will come and have it, the table is spread and loaded for you. Even more, "the word is nigh thee, even in thy mouth."[27]

What! Is the bread of life *in your mouth*, and you will not eat it? Poor, hungry, empty, needy sinner, can you reject what God puts into your mouth? If angels will rejoice when you repent, you can be sure there is joy in store also for you. Come then to Jesus just as you are. Bring no money with you, bring no qualification with you, and bring no fancied goodness with you. Bring your undeserving self and your sin, and lay them before your Lord. Bring your hard heart, your lack of feeling, your lack of grace, and just come and find all that you want in Christ, who is waiting to bless you.

When I was a child, I remember a school festival where the children were instructed to bring their own mugs with them. Now that showed the poverty of those who gave the treat; but my Master does not want you to bring anything; He supplies everything. Come as you are, with nothing except your needs and your willingness to be saved. When an empty, guilty, lost, undone, ruined creature is coming to a great, blessed, and mighty Savior, all he has to think of is the love that invites him and the greatness of the Redeemer who will receive him. Come, you who mourn over sin, or mourn that you cannot mourn, and by believing in Jesus you shall obtain the oil of joy, and the days of your mourning shall be ended.

CHAPTER 6

The Garment of Praise

The garment of praise for the spirit of heaviness...— *Isaiah 61:3d*

We have not yet exhausted the list of comforts that the Anointed has prepared for His mourners. He seems delighted to give a very cloud of blessings "according to the multitude of His tender mercies."[1] Grace, like its God, delights to be a trinity.

This is the third of His sacred exchanges—"the garment of praise for the spirit of heaviness." This is also the broadest of the blessings; for whereas the first adorned the face with beauty, and the second anointed the head with joy, this last and widest covers the whole person with a garment of praise.

Man's first garment was of his own making, and it could not cover his shame; but this garment is of God's making, and it makes us comfortable in ourselves and comely in the sight of God and man. Those to whom God gives the garment of praise are better adorned than Solomon in all his glory. May the blessed Spirit sweetly help us to bring out the rich meaning of this promise to mourners; for, again, I must remind you that these things are only given to them, and not to the thoughtless world.

We have noticed already the variety of the consolation that Jesus brings to mourners. He, the Plant of Renown, produces many lovely flowers with rich perfume and a multitude of choice fruits of delicate taste. Now we would call your attention to their marvelous adaptation to our needs. Man has a spirit, and the gifts of grace are spiritual; his chief maladies lie in his soul, and the blessings of the covenant deal with his spiritual wants.

Our text mentions "the spirit of heaviness," and gives a promise that it shall be removed. The blessings that Jesus gives to us are not surface ones, yet they touch the center of our being. At first, we may not perceive their depth, but only know that beauty is given instead of ashes. This might seem to be an external change. Further on, however, joy is given instead of mourning, and this is inward. The thought has advanced, and we are getting nearer the heart. However, in the words before us, the very spirit of heaviness—the fountain from where the mourning flows, the hearth upon which the ashes are burned—is dealt with and taken away. In its place, we receive the garment of praise.

What a mercy it is that the blessings of the everlasting covenant belong to the realm of the spirit: after all, the outward is transient, and the visible soon perishes. We are grateful for the food and raiment that our bodies require; but our more severe need is nourishment, consolation, and protection for our spirits. The covenant of grace blesses the man himself, the soul, which is the essence of his life. It puts away the sordid sackcloth of despondency, and robes the spirit in royal garments of praise.

Judge your condition by the value you put upon such favors. For, if you have learned to prize them, they are yours. The worldly person cares nothing for spiritual blessings; his beauty, and joy, and praise are found in things that perish in the using. But those who know their preciousness have been taught of God. Therefore, since they can appreciate them, they shall have them. Soul-mercy is the very soul of mercy, and he whom the Lord blesses in his spirit is blessed indeed.

I want you still further to notice how these blessings grow as we proceed. At first, out of the triplet of favors here bestowed, there was *beauty given instead of ashes*. There is much there: beauty of personal character before God is no insignificant thing. A man might have that and, due to his anxiety of heart, he might scarcely be aware of it. Doubtless, many who are lovely in the sight of God spend much of their time in bewailing their own uncomeliness. Many a saint sorrows over himself while others are rejoicing in him.

Therefore, the next mercy given to the mourner in Zion is the *oil of joy*, which is a personal and conscious delight. The man rejoices. He perceives that he is made beautiful before God, and he begins to joy in what the Lord has done for him, and in the Anointed One from whom the oil of gladness descends. This is an advance upon the other, but now we come to the highest of all.

Seeing that God has made him glad, the mourner perceives his obligations to God; he expresses them in thankfulness. He stands before the Most High like a white-robed priest, putting on *praise as the garment* in which he appears in the courts of the Lord's house and is seen by his brethren.

As you advance in the divine life, the blessings you receive will appear to be greater and greater. Some promising things become small by degrees and miserably less; however, in the kingdom of heaven we go from strength to strength. The beginning of the Christian life is like the water in the pots at Cana, yet, in due time it blushes into wine.

The pathway we tread is at first as bright as the dawn; yet, if we pursue it with sacred perseverance, then its refulgence will be as the perfect day. There shall be no going down of our sun, but it shall shine with increasing luster till it shall be as the light of seven days; and the days of our mourning shall be ended.

I beg you also to mark that when we reach the greatest mercy and stand on the summit of blessing, we have reached a condition of *praise*: praise to God invests our whole nature. To be wrapped in praise to God is the highest state of the soul. To receive the mercy for which we praise God is something, but to be wholly clothed with praise to God for the mercy received is far more.

Why, praise is heaven, and heaven is praise! To pray is heaven below, but praise is the essence of heaven above. When you bow lowest in adoration, you are at your very highest. The soul full of joy takes a still higher step when it clothes itself with praise. Such a heart takes to itself no glory, for it is dressed in gratitude, and so hides itself. Nothing is seen of the flesh and its self-exaltation, since the garment of praise hides the pride of man.

May all of you who are heavy in spirit be so clothed with delight in the Lord, who has covered you with the robe of righteousness, so that you may be as wedding guests adorned for the palace of the King with glittering garments of adoring love.

Looking carefully into the words before us, we will dwell, first, upon the *spirit of heaviness*; secondly, upon *the promise implied in the text—that this shall be removed*; and then, thirdly, upon *the garment of praise that is to be bestowed.*

I. First, let us reflect upon THE SPIRIT OF HEAVINESS. We would not make this meditation doleful, and yet it may be well to set forth the night side of the soul. Thereby, we may show in a better way a sympathetic spirit, and come more truly home to those who are in heaviness through manifold temptations.

Some of us know by experience what the spirit of heaviness means. It comes upon us at times even now. There are many things in the body, there are many things in the family, and there are many things in daily life that make us sad. Facts connected with the past and with the future cause us at times to hang our heads.

We shall now dwell upon those former times when we were under the spirit of heaviness because of unpardoned sin. We cannot forget that we were in bondage in a spiritual Egypt. We would awaken our memories to remember the wormwood and the gall, the place of dragons and of owls.

Observe that this heaviness is an inward matter, and it is usually a grief that a man tries to keep to himself. It is not that he is sick in body, though his unbelieving friends imagine that he must surely be ailing, or he would not seem so melancholy. They say, "He sits alone and keeps silent." They say that he has a depression upon him. They invite him out into their company, and try to joke him out of his distress.

The fact is: sin is pressing upon him, and well may the spirit be heavy when it has that awful load to carry. Day and night God's hand also is heavy upon him, and well may his spirit be loaded down. Conviction of sin makes us as a cart that is loaded with sheaves, but it is intensely inward and, therefore, not to be understood by careless minds. "The heart knoweth its own bitterness, and a stranger intermeddleth not therewith."[2] I have known persons who have been the subject of this heaviness, who most diligently endeavor to conceal from others even the slightest appearance of it, and I cannot say that there has not been some wisdom in so doing, for ungodly men despise those who tremble at the word of God. What do they care about sin? They can sin and rejoice in it as the swine can roll in the mire and feel itself at home.

Those who weep in secret places, because the arrows of the Lord have wounded them, are shunned by those who forget God, and they need not be sorry for it, since such company can furnish no balm for their wounds. Mourner, you are wise to keep your sorrow to yourself, so far as the wicked are concerned; remember, though perhaps you do not think so, there are hundreds of God's children who know all about your condition. If you could be bold enough to open your mind to them and tell them of your heaviness of spirit, you would be surprised to find how thoroughly they would sympathize with you, and how accurately some of them could describe the maze through which you are wandering.

All are not tender of heart, but there are believers who would enter into your experience, and who might by God's blessing give you the clue to the labyrinth of your grief. The Lord comforted Paul by Ananias, and you may be sure that there is an Ananias for you.[3]

If you feel, as many do, that you could not unburden your soul to your parents or relatives, go to some other experienced believers, and, as far as you can, tell them your painful condition. I know, for I have felt the same. You feel that all hope of being saved is taken away and that you are utterly prostrate; yet, there is hope.

While this heaviness is inward, notice that it is *real.* Heaviness of spirit is one of the most terribly true of all our griefs. He who is cheerful and light-hearted too often scorns and ridicules him who is sad of soul. He calls him "nervous," "fanciful," "almost out of his mind," "very excitable," "quite a monomaniac," and so on—the current idea being that there is really no need for alarm, and that sorrow for sin is mere fanaticism. If some persons had suffered half an hour of conviction of sin themselves, they would look with different eyes upon those who feel the spirit of heaviness. I say it, and I know what I am saying: next to the torment of hell itself, there is only one sorrow more severe than that of a broken and a contrite spirit that trembles at God's word and yet does not dare to suck comfort out of it—the bitterness of remorse and despair. It is unspeakably heartbreaking to bow at the mercy seat and to fear that no answer will ever come, to lie at the feet of Jesus but to be afraid to look up to Him for salvation. To be conscious of nothing but abounding sin and raging unbelief, and to expect nothing but sudden destruction—this is an earthly Tophet.[4]

There are worse wounds than those that torture the flesh, and more cruel pangs arise from the broken bones of the soul than from those of the body. Sharp is that cut which goes to the very heart and yet does not kill, but makes men wish that they could die or cease to be. There is a prison that no iron bars can make, and a fetter such as no smith can forge. Sickness is a trifle compared to it; to some men it is less endurable than the rack or the stake. To be impaled upon your own sins, pilloried by your own conscience, shot at by your own judgment, as with barbed arrows—this is anguish and torment.

This heaviness of spirit puts a weight upon the man's activity, and clogs him in all things. He who bears the weight of sin is weighted heavily. You put before him the precious promises, but he does not understand them, for the heaviness presses upon his mental faculties. You assure him that these promises are meant for him, but he cannot believe you, for heaviness of spirit palsies the grasping hand by which he might appropriate the blessing.

"Their soul abhoreth all manner of meat; and they draw near unto the gates of death."[5] Troubled minds at times lose all their appetite. They need spiritual food, and yet turn from it. They are afraid to feed upon the most wholesome meat of the gospel, for their sadness makes them fearful of presumption. Heaviness brings on amazement, and this is but another word for saying that the mind is in a maze, and cannot find its way out.

They are weighted as to their understanding and their faith, for "the spirit of heaviness" presses there also. Their memory, too, is quick enough at recollecting sin, but to anything that might minister comfort it is strangely weak; even as Jeremiah said, "Thou hast removed my soul far off from peace: I forget prosperity."[6] Indeed, David was more oblivious still, for he says, "My heart is smitten, and withered like grass; so that I forget to eat my bread."[7]

All the faculties become dull and inert, and the man is like one in a deadly swoon. I have heard persons under conviction of sin say, "I seem absolutely stupid about divine things." Like one that is stunned by a severe blow, they fall down, and scarcely know what they feel or do not feel. Were they in their clear senses we could set the gospel before them, and point out the way of salvation, and they would soon lay hold of it; but, alas, they seem to have no capacity to understand the promise or to grasp its consolation.

I remember once speaking to a captain who was distressed of mind, as we were sailing down a river. When I spoke about the many promises of the Word, he replied, "You see those great mooring-posts along shore?"

"Yes." I saw them clearly enough.

"Well," he said, "it is a very easy thing, you know, to moor a ship when you once get the rope round those posts, but I cannot throw the line or fasten the hawser, and so I drift down the stream. I know the promises would hold me well enough, but I cannot hitch the rope round one of them."

Yes, *there* is the difficulty. When men reel to and fro, and stagger like a drunken man, and are at their wits' end in the midst of a sea of soul-trouble, you may tell them, "There is the harbor," but they are befogged, and cannot see it. You ask them if they cannot see the red lights. Yes, they can, but they appear to dance before their eyes, and they cannot put the ship about. How sad, this heaviness of spirit!

Now, this heaviness of spirit also renders everything around the man heavy. The external is generally painted from within. A merry heart makes mirth in the dull September fog under a leaden sky, but a dull heart finds sorrow amidst May blossoms and June flowers. A man colors the world he lives in to the tint of his own soul. "Things are not what they seem"; yet what they seem has often more influence upon us than what they are.

Given a man, then, with heaviness of spirit, you will find that his sorrows appear to be greater than he can bear. The commonplace worries of life, which cheerfulness sports with, are a load to a sad heart; yes, the grasshopper is a burden. The ordinary duties of life become weariness, and slight domestic cares are torture. He trembles, lest he should commit sin even in going in and out of his house. A man who bears the weight of sin has small strength for any other load.

Even the joys of life become somber. It matters not how much God has blessed a man in his family, in his daily provisions, or in his storehouse. For, as long as his heart is oppressed and his soul bowed down with sin, what are the bursting barns, and what are the overflowing wine vats to him? He pines for a peace and rest that these things cannot yield. If the eye be dark, then the sun itself affords no light.

There is one thing, however, which we would say to mourners pressed down with guilt: whatever heaviness you feel it is no greater heaviness than sin ought to bring upon a man, for it is an awful thing to have sinned against God. If the sense of sin should drive you to distraction—and quibblers often say that religion does this—it might reasonably do so, if there were no other matters to think upon, no forgiving love and atoning blood. That which is the result of sin ought not to be charged upon religion.

But, true religion should be praised, because it brings relief to all this woe. Sin is the most horrible thing in the universe. When a man sees how foully he has transgressed, it is no wonder that he is greatly troubled.

To think that I—a creature that God has made, which He could crush as easily as a moth—have dared to live in enmity to Him for many years, and have even become so hardened as to forget Him, and perhaps defy Him. This is terrible.

When I have been told of His great love, I have turned on my heel and rejected it. Yes, and when I have even seen that love in the bleeding body of His dear Son, I have been unbelieving and have ignored boundless grace, and gone from bad to worse, greedy after sin.

Is it a wonder that, when men have seen the guilt of all this, they have felt their moisture turned into the drought of summer and cried in desperation, "My soul chooses strangling rather than life"?

However low you are, beloved mourner, you are not exaggerating your guilt. Apart from the grace of God, your case is indeed as hopeless as you suppose. Though you lie in the very dust and dare not look up, the position is not lower than you ought to take. You richly deserve the anger of God, and when you have some sense of what that wrath must be, you are not more fearful of it than you should be, for it is a fearful thing to fall into the hands of the living God. "He toucheth the hills, and they smoke." [8]

> The pillars of heaven's starry roof
> Tremble and start at His reproof.

What will His wrath be when He puts on His robes of justice and comes forth to mete out justice to the rebellious? O God, how terrible is Your wrath! Easily might we be crushed at the very thought of it.

Another reflection we would suggest here: if you have great heaviness of spirit because of sin, you are by no means alone in it, for some of the best servants of God have endured hard struggling before they have found peace with God. Read their biographies, and you will find that even those who have really believed in Christ have at some time or other felt the burden of sin pressing with intolerable weight upon their souls. Some of them have recorded their experience in terrifying sentences, and others have not dared to commit to writing what they have felt.

"Weeping-cross," as the old writers call it, is a much-frequented spot. Many roads meet at that point, and most pilgrims have left a pool of tears there.

There is this also to be added. Your Lord and Master, He to whom you must look for hope, knew what heaviness meant on account of sin. He had no sin of His own, but He bore the iniquity of His people, and hence He was prostrate in Gethsemane. We read, "He began to be sorrowful and to be very heavy."[9] The spirit of heaviness was upon Him, and He sweat, as it were, great drops of blood falling to the ground.

This same heaviness made Him cry upon the tree, "My God, my God, why hast thou forsaken me?"[10] Jesus was sore amazed and very heavy. To Him, as passing through that awful heaviness, I would bid you look in your hour of terror, for He alone is your door of hope. Through His heaviness yours shall be removed, for "the chastisement of our peace *was* upon him; and with his stripes we are healed."[11]

II. And now, secondly, let us see THE HEAVINESS REMOVED, for this text contains a divine promise: the anointed Savior will take it away. Only a word or two upon this.

Brethren, do you ask how Jesus removes the spirit of heaviness? We answer, He does it thus—by revealing to us with clearness and certainty that our sin is pardoned. The Holy Spirit brings us to trust in Christ, and the inspired word assures us that Christ suffered in the room, place, and stead of all believers.

Therefore, we perceive that He died for us and that nothing remains for us to suffer, because sin, having been laid upon the Substitute, is no more upon us. We rejoice in the fact of our Lord's substitution and the transfer of our sins to Him. We see that if He stood in our place, then we stand in His, and if He was rejected, we then are "accepted in the beloved."[12] Immediately, this spirit of heaviness disappears, because the reason for it is gone.

> I will praise you every day!
> Now your anger's turn'd away,
> Comfortable thoughts arise
> From the bleeding sacrifice.

Moreover, in the new birth the Holy Spirit infuses into us a new nature, and that new nature does not know the spirit of heaviness. It is a thing of light and life and joy in the Holy Spirit. The newborn nature looks up and perceives its kinship with God. It rejoices in the favor of the Holy One, from whom it came. It rests in the Lord. Yes, it joys and rejoices in Him; whereas the old sin-spirit still sinks us down according to its power—as we still have the evil heart of unbelief—this new life wells up within us as a living fount of crystal. It buoys us up with the peace and joy that come of the Holy Spirit's indwelling. Thus, the inner life becomes a constant remedy for heaviness of spirit.

Faith, too, that blessed gift of God, works to the clearing away of heaviness, wherever it resides. Faith sings, "All things are mine, why should I sorrow? All my sin is gone, why should I pine and moan? All things as to the present life are supplied me by the God of providence and grace, and the future is guaranteed to me by the covenant, in all things ordered and sure."

Faith takes the telescope, looks beyond the narrow range of time into the eternal heavens, and sees a crown laid up for the faithful. Yes, and her ears are opened so that she hears the songs of the redeemed by blood before the throne. Thus, she bears away the spirit of heaviness. If I see no joy with these poor eyes, then faith has other eyes with which she discovers rivers of delight. If flesh and blood give me nothing but causes for dismay, then faith knows more and sees more, and she perceives causes for overflowing gratitude and delight.

Hope enters, too, with her silver light, borrowed from faithful promises. She expects the future glory, at which we hinted just now, and begins to anticipate it all; so, again, she drives away the gloom of the heart.

Love, also, the sweetest of the three, comes in and teaches us to be resigned to the will of God, and then sweetly charms us into acquiescence with all the divine purposes. When we reach that point—and so love God that whatever He may do with us we are resolved to trust Him and praise His name—then the spirit of heaviness must vanish.

Now, beloved mourners, I trust you know what this great uplifting means. It is a work in which the Lord is greatly glorified when He raises a poor, begrimed soul out of the sordid potsherds among which it has lain, and gives it to soar aloft as on the silver wings of a dove. Some of us can never forget the hour of our great deliverance. It was the day of our espousals, the time of love, and it must forever remain as the beginning of days unto us. All glory be to Him who has loosened our bonds and set our feet in a large room.

III. But now we come to the third and most prominent point of the text, THE GARMENT OF PRAISE BESTOWED, which takes the place of the spirit of heaviness. We suppose this may mean, and probably does mean, that the Lord gives us a garment that is honorable and worthy of praise: and what is this garment but the righteousness of our Lord Jesus Christ?

The Lord arrays His poor people in a robe that causes them no longer to be worthy of shame, but fit to be praised. They become not guilty in His sight. What a blessing this is! Did not the father, when he received the prodigal, say, "Bring forth the best robe and put it on him"?[13] That was a garment of praise instead of the spirit of heaviness. Whenever a child of God begins to perceive his adoption and to say, "Abba, Father," then he puts on a garment suitable for a child to wear, an honorable dress, a garment of praise.

When we realize that Christ has made us priests unto God, and we therefore put on the priestly garment of sanctification by beginning to offer the sacrifice of prayer and praise, then, again, we wear a garment of praise.

When we exercise the high prerogative of kings—for we are kings as well as priests—then, again, we wear not a sordid vesture of dishonor, nor the costume of a prison house, nor the rags of beggary, nor the black robe of condemnation, but a garment of honor and of praise.

Every child of God should be clothed with the garments of salvation: his Savior has prepared them for this end. Let him wrap them about him and be glad, for these garments make him beautiful in the sight of God.

But I choose, rather, to follow the exact words of our version and to speak of the garment of praise as meaning gratitude, thanksgiving, and adoration. The anointed Comforter takes away the spirit of heaviness, and He robes His people in the garment of praise.

Now, this is something outward as well as inward. A wise man endeavors to hide the heaviness of his spirit. But, when the Lord takes that away from him, he does not wish to conceal his gratitude. I could not help telling those I lived with when I found the Lord.

Master John Bunyan informs us that he was so anxious to let someone know of his conversion that he wanted to tell the crows on the ploughed land all about it. I do not wonder. It is a piece of news that it would be hard to withhold. Whenever a man's inward heaviness is graciously removed, he puts on the outward manifestation of joy, and walks abroad in the silken robes of praise.

As we have already said, a garment is a thing that covers a man. So, when a man learns to thank God aright, his praise covers him. He himself is hidden while he gives all the glory to God. The man is seen as clothed in praise from head to foot.

When Christians begin to speak of the love and mercy of God to them, many persons very unfairly judge them, and cry out that they are egotistical. But how can it be egotistical to talk of what the Lord has done for you? If you speak with any sort of confidence, faultfinders say that you are presumptuous. How can it be presumptuous to believe what God Himself declares? It is presumptuous to doubt what God says, but it is no presumption to believe God. Neither is it egotism to state the truth.

If I were to say that God has not blessed me abundantly, the pulpit on which I stand would cry out against me. Shall I conceal the mercy of God, as if it were stolen goods? Never. Rather, I will speak the more boldly of the measureless love that has kept my soul from going down to the pit. "He that glorieth, let him glory in the Lord."[14]

Bless the Lord, O you saints of His, and give thanks to His holy name. Show forth His salvation, compel men to see it, gird it about your loins, and wear it for your adorning in all companies.

While speaking of this garment of praise, first let us enquire, *of what is it made?*

In a large measure, is not praise composed of an attentive observation of God's mercy? Thousands of blessings come to us without our knowledge. We take them in at the back door and put them away in the cellar. Now praise takes note of them, preserves the invoice of favors received, and records the goodness of the Lord. O, friends, if you do this, you will never be short of reasons for praise. He who notices God's mercy will never be without a mercy to notice. This is the chief material of the garment of praise: attentive consideration of divine grace is the broadcloth out of which the garment of praise is made.

The next thing is grateful memory. Very much that God does for us we bury alive in the grave of oblivion. We receive His mercies as if they were common trash. They are no sooner come than they are gone, and the proverb truly says, "Bread eaten is soon forgotten." My brethren, the Lord may give you a thousand favors, and you will not praise Him. Yet, if He smites you with one little stroke of the whip, you grumble at Him. You write His mercies on the water, and your own trials you engrave on granite. These things ought not to be. Maintain the memory of His great goodness. "Forget not all his benefits."[15] Call to remembrance your song in the night. Remember the loving-kindnesses of the Lord. In this also we find rich material for the garment of praise.

We are further aided by rightly estimating mercy. Is it not a great mercy to be alive and not in hell, to be in your senses and not in a mental institution, to be in health and not in the hospital, to be in one's own room and not in the workhouse? These are great favors, and yet, perhaps, we seldom thank God for them. Add up your spiritual mercies, if you can. Remember on the other hand what you deserved and what it cost the Savior to bring these blessings to you. Remember how patient the Lord has been with your refusal of His love, and how continuously He has loaded you with benefits. Weigh His mercies as well as count them, and they will help you to put on the garment of praise.

It is the telling out of the divine goodness which largely constitutes praise: to observe, to remember, to estimate, to prize, and then to speak of the Lord's gracious gifts—all these are essential. Praise is the open declaration of the gratitude that is felt within. How greatly do many fail in this: if you visit them, how readily they enlarge upon their troubles. In five minutes they have informed you about the damp weather, their aching bones, and their low wages. Others speak of the bad times and the decline of trade, until you know their song by heart.

Is this the manner of the people of God? Should we not regale our guests with something better than the bones of our meat and the hard crusts of our bread? Let us set before them good tidings, and cheerfully tell of the divine goodness to us, lest they should go away under the impression that we serve a hard master.

It would create an almost miraculous change in some people's lives if they made a point of speaking most of the precious things and least of the worries and ills. Why always the poverty? Why always the pains? Why always the dying child? Why always the husband's small wages? Why always the unkindness of a friend? Why not sometimes—yes, why not always—the mercies of the Lord? That is praise, and it is to be our everyday garment, the special attire of every servant of Christ.

Second, *who ought to wear this garment*? The answer may be suggested by another question: whom does it fit? Truly there is a garment of praise that exactly suits *me*, and I mean to wear it on my own person. It is so capacious that some of my brethren would wonder if they could see it spread out. I am so much in debt to my God that, do what I will, I can never give a fair acknowledgement of it. I freely confess that I owe Him more than any man living and am morally bound to praise Him more earnestly than anyone else.

Did I hear some of you claiming to be equal debtors? Do you demand to be allowed to praise Him more than I? Well, I will not quarrel with you. Let the matter stand, and if you will excel me I will praise my Lord for it. Once, while preaching, I remarked that if I entered heaven, then I would take the lowest place, feeling that I owe more to God's grace than anybody else. But when I left the pulpit, I found that I had several competitors who would not yield the lowest place to me. They were each one ready to exclaim—

Then loudest of the crowd *I'll* sing,
While heaven's resounding mansions ring
With shouts of sovereign grace.

Blessed be God, this is the only contention among the birds of paradise—which owes the most, which shall love the best, which shall lie lowest, and which shall extol their Lord the most zealously. Charming rivalry of humility! Let us have more of it below.

I again say there is a garment of praise that fits me. Brother, is there not one that fits you exactly, suiting your state and condition? If you are an heir of heaven, then there is, there must be, a garment of praise that will rest most becomingly upon your shoulders, and you should put it on at once.

Third, *when shall we wear it?* We should certainly appear in it on high days and holidays. On Sabbath days and communion seasons, the hours are fragrant with grateful memories. I heard of someone who did not attend public worship because his clothes were not fit to come in, and I replied, "What can he mean? Does the Lord care for our outward dress? Let him put on the garment of praise, and he may come and be welcome."

The outer vestments matter little indeed; all garments of that sort are only proofs of our fall and of the need to hide our nakedness in shame. Fine dress is unbecoming in the house of God, especially for those who call themselves "miserable sinners." The best adornment is humility of spirit, the robe of thanksgiving, and the garment of praise. The Lord's Day should always be the happiest day of the week, and the communion should be a little heaven to our souls. "Call the Sabbath a delight, the holy of the LORD, honorable."[16]

These garments of praise should be our continual clothing. If we only praise God on high days and public occasions, then we do no more than hypocrites and Pharisees. Even publicans and sinners will give God a good word when their days are bright. But we must bless Him when the tempest threatens. They will say, "Thank God," when they have fine weather for their pleasures or count up a good day's sales in their shop. Only the child of God will praise the Lord in the dark, while smarting under His rod.

It is the unusual privilege of the true believer to say, "Though He slay me, yet will I trust in him...";[17] "The LORD gave, and the LORD hath taken away; blessed be the name of the LORD."[18] There was grand music in such speech when Job first uttered it. I do not think the angel Gabriel can put so much praise into his song as Job put into that heroic word.

He was covered with sore boils and blains, his children were dead, his wife was grieving him, and his friends tormenting him. Yet, he cried, "Blessed be the name of the Lord." O, keep to that theme, mourners; it is music to the ear of your God. To wear the garments of praise when the cupboard is empty, when the little grave is being dug, when the head is aching and the heart is throbbing, when the ship is sinking or trade is failing—this is the fruit of grace, and it is well pleasing unto the Lord.

We should wear the garment of praise on the most commonplace of days. It should be the peasant's frock, the merchant's coat, the lady's dress, and the servant's gown. It is the best for wear, for comfort, and for beauty, and it never gets out of fashion.

I once knew an old saint, a Methodist, a very quaint, original, rustic, old man, who was celebrated for happiness. When he went out to labor early in the morning, he was always singing as he went along the road. The country people used to call it "tooting to himself." Quietly he hummed a bit of a hymn wherever he was. When he used his spade or his hoe, he worked to the music of his heart, and never murmured when in poverty or became angry when held up to ridicule. I wish we were all as spiritually minded and as full of praise as he.

Bless the Lord! Bless the Lord! When should we not bless Him? We will praise Him when our beds refresh us: blessed be He who kept the night watches. When we put on our clothes in the morning, we will bless His name for giving us food and raiment. When we sit down to breakfast, we will bless the love that has provided a table for us. When we go forth to our work, we will bless the Lord who gives us strength to labor. If we must lie at home sorely sick with fierce pain or slow decay, then let us praise Him who heals and sanctifies all our diseases.

Let us endeavor to display the sweet spirit of thankfulness from the rising of the sun to the going down of the same. Every moment may suggest a new verse of our life-psalm, and may cause us to magnify Him whose mercy endures forever.

Now, lastly, *why should we wear the garment of praise?* We should wear it as we wear other raiment, to keep us warm and comfortable, for there is no such vesture in the world as that of praise. It warms the inmost heart, and sends a glow through the whole man. You may go to Nova Zembla and not freeze in such a robe. In the worst cases and in the most sorrowful plights, wherever you may be, you are proof against outward circumstances when your whole being is wrapped up in praise.

Wear it because it will comfort you. Wear it also because it will distinguish you from others. It will be a uniform to you, and men will know whose servant you are. It will be a regimental dress, and show to which army you belong. It will be a court dress, and manifest to what dignity you have attained. So arrayed, you will bear the tokens of your Lord, who often in the days of His sorrow lifted His eye and heart to heaven and thanked the great Father for His goodness.

You should wear the garment of praise because it honors your Lord, especially if you put it on in the time of trouble; for then even ungodly men inquire, "What makes him so calm, so resigned, so happy? There must be something worth having in the religion which he professes."

Therefore, wear the garment of praise, and never take it off until, having had it cleansed, and renewed, and made completely new, you shall wear it in the courts of heaven forever and ever, adoring, magnifying, and praising Him who has delivered you from the spirit of heaviness and clothed you with the garment of praise. May some poor burdened soul lose its heaviness while thinking over our text, and henceforth wear this kingly robe—the garment of praise. Amen.

CHAPTER 7

Trees of Righteousness

...that they might be called trees of righteousness,
the planting of the LORD, that he might be glorified.
—*Isaiah 61:3*e

We have now come to our last discourse upon this choice passage. May those who have been mourning enter into the spirit of the text and forget themselves in the glory of God. This is the near way to the surest comfort. When our one, all-absorbing desire is the glory of God, we rise out of ourselves, and sorrow grows light. May the Holy Spirit, the Comforter, raise us to this state of heart.

The main end and object of the whole system of grace is that the Lord might be glorified. This will be the ultimate result of all that God has planned and wrought for the salvation of men. Throughout the whole dispensation of love, His attributes shine forth in their meridian splendor: His mercy in forgiving the guilty, His justice in the death of their Substitute, His truth in fulfilling His threatening, and His faithfulness in keeping His promise—all will be made manifest to the admiring eyes of the intelligent universe.

The brightest beams of Jehovah's perfect nature might never have been perceived if sin had not entered upon the scene; but Eden's fall and Calvary's redemption have given scope and occasion for the display of divine pity, mercy, justice, and truth. The Lord has an eye to this fact. Since no motive could be found in us, the Lord deals well with us for His own sake, to manifest His own glory.

For this end He has chosen His people: "Having predestinated us unto the adoption of children by Jesus Christ to himself, according to the good pleasure of his will, To the praise of the glory of his grace, wherein he hath made us accepted in the beloved";[1] for this He has called them, "that he might make known the riches of his glory."[2]

For this He preserves, upholds, sustains, sanctifies, and perfects all those whom His sovereign grace has favored: "To the intent that now unto the principalities and powers in heavenly places might be known by the church the manifold wisdom of God."[3]

The passage before us declares that to glorify Jehovah the Spirit of God rested upon our Lord, and for this cause mourners are the objects of His mercy, and prisoners and broken-hearted ones are the witnesses of His saving power. Let us now consider that when the saved ones are delivered from their sorrows and so filled with grace that they are called "trees of righteousness, the planting of the LORD," it is still with this in view, "that he might be glorified."

I. In the first place, much of the glory of grace is seen in the choice of such lowly persons to become partakers of heavenly blessings. THEIR HUMBLE ESTATE commends the love that chose them to be made "trees of righteousness." The choice of men from the dungeon and the ash pit displays the absolute sovereignty and boundless pity of the Lord.

In thinking it over, we may well feel as our great Lord and Master did when He said, "I thank thee, O Father, Lord of heaven and earth, because thou hast hid these things from the wise and prudent, and hast revealed them unto babes. Even so, Father; for so it seemed good in thy sight."[4] The Lord might have chosen to execute His works of grace upon the kings and princes of the earth; instead, He pours contempt upon princes.

As one and another of the Alexanders and Caesars pass before us, we hear a Voice saying, "Look not on his countenance, or on the height of his stature; because I have refused him."[5] Had these been the sole objects of election, human pride would have imputed their salvation to the superiority of their descent or the loftiness of their rank: therefore this shall not be.

If the Lord had chosen sages and philosophers, if it had been necessary to pass through various grades of scholarship in order to obtain the favor of God, then human learning would have been considered the cause of holiness, and the university would have monopolized the glory. This also shall not be. Neither can riches sway the choice of heaven, nor personal beauty, nor courage, nor favor among men. Grace, and grace alone, must reign and lift the mourners from the dunghill, while the haughty sons of pride are passed by.

Moreover, the Lord has not made His selection according to natural character; for if He had in every case chosen those who have been excellent in morals from their youth up, then the honor would have been ascribed to good works, and grace would have been elbowed out of the throne. If the good Shepherd had come only to watch over the ninety and nine that did not stray, and not to seek lost sheep, then it would have been said, "After all, these saved ones owe but little to mercy, for their admirable character lies at the root of it all." It is all very well to talk of grace, but what sort of grace is it that comes only to the most deserving?

In such a case, the mercy of God would have received no honor; yet, as we read the passage before us, we see that the choice of God was not directed by any consideration of personal deservings, and we are led to adore the Lord in His condescending love.

The divine choice is not such as to manifest the goodness of man—alas! where is it? Nor the wisdom of man—what is it? Nor the greatness of man—where can it be found? Rather, it is to manifest the greatness, the wisdom, and the grace of God, that thereby "he might be glorified." What a mine of comfort is hidden in this fact! Mourners in

Zion who lament their own unworthiness should remember this and be encouraged.

Now, note well that the anointed Savior came to bless those who are *of a meek and unpretending spirit*—"The LORD hath anointed me to preach good tidings unto the meek," which Luke renders, "to the poor." Both expressions point at the same class of persons: those who are despised by others and who look upon themselves with small esteem; persons who have lowly thoughts and consider themselves quite unworthy of a glance from the eye of God. These meek ones of the earth never think of standing in the center of the temple to thank God that they are not as other men; rather, they take their places in any out-of-the-way corner, smite on their breasts, and confess that they are sinners. Our Savior came to bless these lowly minded ones, because He knows that they will never advance a claim to the honor of their own salvation. They know themselves too well to dream of boasting, and nobody in the world will ever think of rendering honor to them, for they are despised by their fellows. In the choice of such persons, the Lord's end is answered, "that he might be glorified."

Furthermore, the Lord has chosen those who *are broken-hearted*. When persons are very low in circumstances, they may, nevertheless, possess great force of character and wonderful courage, by means of which they may force their way to the front. But, the persons who are interested in the blessings that Jesus came to bestow are not described as being of this brave and resolute race; for it is written, "He hath sent me to bind up the broken-hearted." He is sent to encourage those whose spirit fails them.

As for the self-confident, who say, "I may be very poor in spiritual matters, but I can soon make myself better, and lay up a heap of religious wealth," nothing whatever is promised to them; but the broken-down ones, who are crushed in spirit and wounded in heart, are specially spoken of. These feel that if they ever rise, then it must be God alone who can raise them, for they have no strength left; they are among the first to confess that if they are ever brought to heaven, then it will be a miracle of divine power and grace.

As for themselves, each of these broken hearts cries, "My strength is dried up like a potsherd. I scarcely feel power to pray, or even to think a good thought. Where shall I find foundation for hope? What can I expect but wrath?" The Lord Jesus is anointed to bind up such broken-spirited ones as these; and He will derive unmingled praise from their grateful hearts, since their natural condition excludes all boasting, and their deep and conscious obligations to grace will ensure their magnifying the Lord as long as they live.

> Perish each thought of human pride,
> Let God alone be magnified;
> His glory let the heavens resound,
> Shouted from earth's remotest bound.

If a poor man has but little spirit, yet there is always hope for him while he has his liberty; however, those whom the Lord blesses *are in bonds.* A brave heart says, "Set me free, and I will hope for some turn of the tide." However, what shall the captive do? There are, doubtless, men who believe that they are, by nature, morally free, and they are always glorying in the freedom of their wills. They do not believe for a moment that free will is a slave, as some of us know it to be; rather, they glory in the dignity of their nature and the soundness of their judgment. They are persuaded that they are able, whenever they think fit, to climb to any moral or spiritual elevation they may desire.

These are not the persons, however, whom the Anointed comes to bless, for they are described as captives, bound in prison. The objects of divine grace feel that when they would do good, evil is present with them. They admit that they dare not trust their own understanding, for it is too much a captive to ignorance and prejudice; neither do they dare to obey their own will, for it is obstinate and perverse. Nor may they indulge their own heart, for it is naturally enthralled by sin and Satan, and even when delivered carries about with it the marks of its fetters.

These are the people to whom our Lord proclaims liberty, so that, when they are emancipated, they may not be able to glory in themselves in even the slightest degree; for they cannot pride themselves in their freedom, since it was a pure gift procured for them by Another's hand when they themselves could not move hand or foot to procure it, seeing they were bound in chains that they could not break. In their case also, the design of God's grace is answered, "that he might be glorified."

Besides that, these people whom the Lord chose to glorify Him were *bowed down with sorrow.* They are described as having ashes on their heads and heaviness in their hearts. These feel the burden of sin, and are crushed under a sense of the wrath of God, which they have consciously deserved. And if through rich mercy they at length find forgiveness, they are certain to ascribe the work of salvation to God alone. They will be clear and sound upon the doctrines of grace.

We have almost wished that certain preachers who are very indistinct in their teachings as to the grace of God had suffered a little of the self-abasement and self-despair that have fallen to the lot of many saints. Lack of law-work in the heart is at the bottom of much mingle-mangle doctrine. If cloudy teachers had felt more of the plague of their own hearts, they would be more clear in their declaration that we are saved by grace "through faith; and that not of ourselves: it is the gift of God."[6] Salvation is of the Lord from first to last. It is not of man, neither by man; it is not of the will of man, nor of blood, nor of birth, nor of outward ordinances, nor of anything, but of the sovereign will and power of God alone.

What does the Scripture say? "I *am* the LORD: that is my name: and my glory I will not give to another."[7] Let me, therefore, beseech all who have tasted the love of God to make this point as clear as the sun whenever they speak to others, and to make it plain to their own hearts, since to rob

God of His honor is treason-felony against the majesty of heaven.

As for myself, I protest that I cannot put my finger upon anything in my whole life for which I dare take the least credit before God. Truly, if in any of us there has been any virtue, if there has been any praise, if there has been anything honest or of good repute, if there has been any power in prayer, or usefulness, or consecration, or likeness to Christ, all the honor thereof must be rendered unto the Lord alone. "Not unto us, O LORD, not unto us, but unto thy name give glory, for thy mercy, and for thy truth's sake."[8]

This is the spot of God's children: they all, without exception, render all the honor of their salvation, heartily and unreservedly, to the Lord alone. Thus, the end of eternal love is secured, "that he might be glorified." Mourning friend, what do you say? Is not this method of grace as suitable to you as it is glorifying to the Lord, and do you not cheerfully accept it? I know you do.

II. Compelled by our space to be brief, we now note, secondly, God is glorified in THEIR AFTER CHARACTER; for those poor, humbled, downcast souls become so remarkable in character that the text says they shall "be called trees of righteousness, the planting of the LORD."

Holy Scripture is very fond of comparing good men to trees. In this place it seems to be a somewhat incongruous metaphor; but this may be intentional, in order to call us away from the letter to the inward sense, which is spiritual. If the meaning had been natural and moral, no doubt the figures would have run on in a connected series; but here we leap from one to another, as if to show that the outward and external cannot fully set forth the inner and spiritual.

Let us look into the expression, "trees of righteousness." When men whom God has loved are saved, they are saved in a righteous way. They are "trees *of righteousness*, the planting of the LORD." True, they are saved by sovereign grace, but yet in a righteous way. They are saved by mercy, but they are not called trees of mercy, because righteousness is the greatest marvel in their salvation, and to encompass this the utmost wisdom has been exercised.

In a previous sermon, I tried to show you how, in the life and death of Christ, mercy proclaimed acceptance, and yet justice meted out vengeance; and therefore we see that those whom grace redeems are so saved that they glorify the divine righteousness more than any other beings. It is a wonderful thing that a sinner should be saved righteously, that God should be "just and yet the justifier of him that believeth!"[9]

The grand fact of the substitution of Christ for His people, so that mercy could be exercised without eclipsing justice, is the marvel of eternity. Men may cavil at it, but angels admire it. All down eternity, there will be mighty spirits educated in heaven itself who, notwithstanding their lofty powers, will be lost in wonder at the righteous salvation of God. The redeemed shall forever be signs and wonders to the whole intelligent universe—they shall "be called trees of righteousness," the grandest of all exhibitions of the righteousness of God.

There was a tree of knowledge, and by that we fell; there is a tree of life by which we rise; and we ourselves are now trees of righteousness, the immortal embodiments of the rectitude of our glorious God.

The text, however, means something more: God is glorified in the character of His people, because they become righteous in their lives. It is no small wonder when a great sinner becomes a great saint. Nothing is more interesting or surprising than the phenomenon of conversion: I am sure we do not make enough of it in answering the worldly one. He sneeringly inquires, "Where is your God?"

Our answer may well be—"Here we see Him divinely transforming the nature of men." We have seen hundreds, if not thousands, converted, in whom there has been a change so extraordinary that they themselves would not have believed that such a transmutation could have been accomplished. The work of conversion in many has been so marked that, if the men had actually died and risen again from the dead, they could not have been more completely different from their former selves. We have seen the unchaste become delicate in modesty, the thief scrupulous in honesty, the blasphemer devout in heart, and the man of fierce, impetuous temper meek as a lamb. Surely "this is the finger of God."[10] All things do not continue as they were, for here is a new creation going on before our eyes every day.

The Lord makes the saved ones to be temperate, upright, and gracious, so that men who look on them are compelled to exclaim, "This is the planting of God, and these are trees of righteousness." Those who profess to be converted should remember this, and in all things adorn the doctrine of their God and Savior "that He may be glorified."

What is meant by the expression, "trees of righteousness"? Does it not assure us that the poor and broken-hearted, when renewed by grace, shall flourish like the trees of the forest? Before, they were like the heath in the desert, or like a tree cut down whose stump alone is left; but when Jesus visits them, they exhibit new life and beauty, and rise to a prominence and continuance that are very wonderful. "He shall be like a tree planted by the rivers of water."[11] "For as the days of a tree *are* the days of my people."[12] There is joy on their face, rest in their heart, and peace in their life: the barren soul is revived; in holiness it grows, and in hope it buds.

Does not the expression also teach us that those whom Jesus comforts become fixed and established? Before, you could move them about at your pleasure, for they were likened to "a rolling thing before the whirlwind";[13] but now, they have roots, which hold them firmly, like the oak or the cedar. Rough winds of trial only strengthen their hold, and the jests and slanders of a cruel world cause them to adhere all the more closely to the truth with the very roots of their soul.

What a mercy it is when God gives His people fixity and stability, so that men may call them trees of righteousness! When the saints abide in their steadfastness to the Lord, then is the design accomplished, "that he might be glorified."

Also, like trees these renewed ones yield a pleasant shade of gracious influence over others. Under a tree one shelters himself from the burning heat; and God works so graciously in believers that the poor soul that was once so broken-hearted as to need comfort from others now becomes himself a son of consolation. As a tiny plant he needed to be sheltered with care, but now he has become a tree, and the birds of the air come and lodge in his branches. Young saints gain knowledge, and tried saints obtain consolation from those very persons who a little while ago sat in ashes, bowed down with heaviness. We may think of them while we remember what the poet said of the trees:

> And ye are strong to shelter all meek things;
> All that need home and covert love your shade;
> Birds of shy song, and low-voice quiet springs,
> And nun-like violets, by the wind betray'd.

Now when the Lord does all this, then He is greatly glorified. When the Lord brings His mourners to be like the blessed man in the first Psalm, "a tree planted by the rivers of waters," He receives honor. Never does a growing, flourishing, established, useful believer extol himself; but he lives to show forth the praises of the Lord, to whose right-hand planting he owes everything.

III. We must further observe that the text says they shall "be *called* trees of righteousness": they not only are so, but they shall be called by that name. This also honors God when His people obtain PUBLIC RECOGNITION of their righteous character from both the willing and the unwilling who observe them. Possibly this may aid us in seeing the suitableness of the figure, for certain trees have become famous in connection with events and qualities, as "the oak of weeping,"[14] because

Deborah was buried there, and the Gospel Oak, under which the gospel was preached in the days of the reformers.

Christian men have sometimes become as famous as celebrated trees. For instance, trees have been *landmarks*: the county terminates at the great oak, or the parish boundary is fixed by the ash-grove. In history, trees have been landmarks: the tree of knowledge of good and evil marks the fall; the olive marks the assuagement of the deluge; the tree in Mamre notes the era of Abraham; and the palms of Elim record the age of Moses.

You may divide the ages, if you like, by memorable trees, and evidently, in the same way, you may name succeeding periods by good men who have thus become "trees of righteousness." Eras may be dated from Adam to Enoch, from Noah to Abraham, from Jacob to Moses, from Joshua to David, and so on. May our Lord take some of you who are broken-hearted and sorely afflicted and make you so eminently gracious that you may be the landmarks of your age, or at least landmarks in the history of one person and another who shall date their new birth from the hour when you conversed with them.

Some trees are *centers of attraction.* That great tree at Mamre under which God met with Abraham has for ages been the center of a fair; and even so there are some Christians under whose branches their fellow Christians hold high holiday and commerce. I have known aged and afflicted believers to whom the saints of a whole region have gone, in order to hear their good words and observe their Christian patience. Scarcely can you go into one of our villages without hearing of some gracious man or woman in whom all believers take pleasure.

Happy are they who do not divide and scatter, but become rallying points for the faithful, and, therefore, "trees of righteousness." Would you have thought that mourners in Zion could ever have risen to such importance? See what the Holy Spirit has done that the Lord might be glorified. Courage, you mourners, the same shall be done with you.

Trees frequently become *marvels of grandeur.* In the New Forest, I have wondered as I have measured the girth of the grand old giants among beech and oak, which for ages have braved the changeful climate of our isle. There they stand, covering many a woodland with their shade. What a history is embodied in those gnarls and knots and twisted branches! How they tell of stormy nights and days of heavy snow! All over the bark and the boughs, time, with his pencil, has written records of sunshine and tempest.

Now, such is a Christian when God makes him rich in grace: if you could but know him and read him, you would see that he is a mass of history. His virtues are the results of severe trial and the records of sublime joys. All the lines of his face mean something; there is not a scar upon his soul, or a dark memory upon his spirit, or a bright recollection in his mind that does not redound to the glory of God. He is a wonder unto many, and will be such even among the angels of God. As monuments of the power of spiritual life to endure all kinds of trials, believers shall be called "trees of righteousness."

Trees, also, are often *pictures of beauty.* Nothing more adorns a landscape than its trees. If you were to cut down every grove and wood, you would produce a horrible dead level. A tree, symmetrical from its root to its highest branch, awakens high delight in the mind of the tasteful observer. Such is the beauty of the Christian character. If you draw near to one who lives near to God, you will be struck with his loveliness; he is the noblest work of God.

> Green as the leaf, and ever fair,
>   Shall his profession shine;
> While fruits of holiness appear
>   Like clusters on the vine.

All saints are not alike, but they are all beautiful, for as Dr. M'Cosh[15] observes:

> One tree differs from another tree in glory. There is one glory of the oak, which has faced a hundred storms and is

ready for as many more; another glory of the sycamore, that "spreads in gentle pomp its honey'd shade"; another glory of the birch, so graceful in the midst of its maiden tresses; another glory of the elm, throwing out its wide arms as if rejoicing in its strength; and another glory of the lime, with its sheltered shade inviting us to enter and to linger.

All these differ, but they all agree in displaying the glory of their Creator. May such beauty yet adorn every mourning soul, that God may be glorified.

IV. Lastly, it is said in the text that God is glorified, because they are not only called "trees of righteousness," but also "the planting of the LORD": this marks THEIR EVIDENT ORIGIN. Men will say, "This is God's work: we know what they once were, and we now see what they have become, and therefore we are sure that the Lord has been at work upon them." I have known persons so desperately bad, so outrageously wicked that, when they have been converted, their neighbors have said, "Do you mean to say that *he* is a Christian? Then miracles will never cease." As one said of his old father, "I have scarcely known him a day sober since I was born, and if he has become a sober, praying man, then there is something in religion, I am sure."

When the Lord chooses a ringleader among sinners, and saves him, His power and grace are undeniably demonstrated. When the proud man is humbled, when the careless boaster becomes serious, when the argumentative infidel prays, when the persecutor preaches, then men say, "This is the planting of the Lord," and the Most High is glorified.

And, dear friends, when Christians rise to a high degree of grace, and exhibit a gracious character in the common walks of life—especially in times of temptation and trial—then, again, men say, "These are trees of the Lord's planting." When a man discovers that you will not yield to temptation though you might be a great gainer by it, when he sees that you do not lose your temper, but are patient under insult, when he sees you do what it is not ordinary for human nature to do, then he is convinced, and in his conscience praises God.

I pray you, then, beloved, if you are indeed the elect of God, in all things endeavor to show the power of the grace that dwells in you. Compel the world to glorify the Lord, who has done such great things for you. You have the promise that you shall accomplish this; do not rest until it is fulfilled.

Thus, have we seen the mourner led on from step to step until he becomes a grand living monument to the glory of God. Will it be so in your case, O troubled one? Why should it not be? You are now a mere bramble or thorn, but grace can make you into one of the trees of the Lord, planted in the courts of our God. Why should it not be sought and found by you, *there* and *now?* There is nothing in the word of God to forbid your coming to God in Christ Jesus; yet, there is everything to invite and encourage you.

Why not come at this moment, and commit your soul to Him who is sent and anointed to save the mourning one? In the name of Jesus, I entreat you at this moment to yield yourself unto God and trust in His Son. Do so, and the work of grace is begun in you, and before long you also shall be called one of the "trees of righteousness, the planting of the LORD, that he might be glorified."

Reference Notes

Remarks: Asterisk (*) notes a Bible verse or passage that Mr. Spurgeon closely quoted from the *KJV* or paraphrased in his original discourse text.

Opine Publishing

Opinari [L.] - to think, to reason...to believe

Opine Publishing produces enjoyable and uplifting books with timeless messages of faith in Jesus Christ and biblical principles for living every day.

The Mourner's Comforter by Charles Haddon Spurgeon is Opine Publishing's first undertaking for a little-known book of time-honored quality by an author of well-known Christian works.

To God be the glory in every good work.